Emily,
I'd love to check out
a tape of your show.
Bon Apetite'

Scot Reed

THE
LOEWS HOTELS FAMILY
COOKBOOK

A COLLECTION OF FAVORITE RECIPES
BY THE CHEFS OF LOEWS HOTELS

Edited by Pat Brown

RECIPES tested and adapted by Phyllis Kohn.

ART DIRECTION: Barbara Lee and Julie Golden.

DESIGN: Suka & Friends Design, Inc., New York.

ILLUSTRATION: Juliette Borda.

PHOTOGRAPHY: James Bettinger (*Tim Fields, p. 45*); Pierre Halmaï (*Eric Fraudau, p. 41*); Martha Lochert (*Jim Makinson, p. 21*); Claude Mathieu (*Mario Martel, p. 75*); Mattox Photography (*Evan Percoco, p. 55, John Rocca, p. 27*); Tonda McKay (*Josh Weekley, p. 17*); Sherrie Nickol (*Jed Gidaly, p. 3, John Iachetti, p. 71, Jonathan M. Tisch, p. 1*); Marshall Williams Photography (*James Boyce, p. 7*); Frasier Young (*Alain Giraud, p. 59*). Photonica (pp. 11, 33, 49, 63).

SPECIAL THANKS TO Marian Succoso, Debra Kelman, Kathy Bervar, Marguarite Clark, Sara Harper, Caroline McDaniel, April Sack and Taryn Schneider as well as all the Food and Beverage Directors, their assistants and secretaries of the Loews Hotels family for their help in gathering materials for this book.

In keeping with Loews Hotels' GOOD NEIGHBOR POLICY, a portion of the proceeds from the Loews Hotels Family Cookbook will be donated to Share Our Strength. One of the nation's leading anti-hunger, anti-poverty organizations, Share Our Strength meets immediate demands for food while investing in long-term solutions to hunger and poverty.

CONTENTS

A LETTER FROM JONATHAN TISCH

At Loews Hotels, our goal is to provide a comfortable, friendly, and unpretentious environment where our guests—business travelers or families on vacation—can accomplish their objectives. We strive to achieve this goal in every aspect of our service, especially in our restaurants and lounges, whether the occasion is a business lunch, a romantic dinner for two, a black-tie gala for 500 people, or a hamburger with fries from room service.

As part of our overall philosophy of operating unique hotels that are complementary to their locations and surroundings, we have assembled a talented and creative group of chefs whose food reflects a similar approach. The result is an emphasis on regional flavors and ingredients in creative menu ideas that are responsive both to current trends and to guest preferences.

The following recipes feature a sampling of what you'll find at Loews Hotels, including personal favorites from the chefs and their guests alike. And, since hotels are often places for celebrating special occasions, we've also provided four seasonal menus which are ideal for holiday entertaining.

We hope that you'll use and enjoy the cookbook. And, whenever your travels take you to one of the cities where Loews Hotels are found, we hope you will allow us to offer you our hospitality.

From our family to yours,

Jonathan M. Tisch
President and CEO, Loews Hotels

FOREWORD

I admit it. I love this book. Not only does it reflect the kind of straightforward and ingredient-driven American cooking I prefer, but it comes from a group of talented people with whom I've gotten to spend farmloads of quality time.

These recipes come from Loews Hotels chefs throughout North America, but let's be clear: With gracious hospitality uppermost in mind, each little culinary outing has been carefully tested and adapted for the home cook—or even the chef cooking at home. The dishes from each pro, while generally representative of the region and—sometimes—a season, are not intended to form a complete menu but rather to offer examples of favorite foods to be enjoyed in various ways.

As for those seasonal menus, they include contributions from numerous Loews kitchens and can certainly be plumbed for the occasional holiday fête or spontaneous celebration.

When the call went out for submissions we all got some pleasant surprises: Lots of fish, streamlined grilled dishes, vegetables, and fruit desserts, as might be expected today, but also heartfelt faves like Turkey Breast Stuffed with Wild Mushrooms and Virginia Ham, Crab Cakes, and Sundaes, as well as some homey, satisfying foods for those times when only comfort will do. It seemed a pretty solid reflection of how Americans—Jon Tisch among them—like to eat these days.

This book, the brainchild of Loews Executive Vice President Charlotte St. Martin, famed for her fried chicken, has been a long time on the simmer, but it should certainly give pleasure for a long time to come. Here's hoping you and yours get to enjoy every nibble and sip.

Clark Wolf
New York City
1998

Clark Wolf, the well known food business and restaurant consultant, has had the pleasure of assisting with Loews Hotels Food & Beverage programs since 1989.

THE REGENCY HOTEL

New York, New York

**EXECUTIVE CHEF
JED MILES GIDALY**

Trained in classical French techniques, Chef Gidaly favors cuisine incorporating eclectic influences such as Mediterranean and Asian and emphasizing ingredients and products indigenous to regional American cooking. Chef Gidaly oversees all aspects of dining: **540 Park** restaurant, room service, and banquet and catering functions. He also created the menus for **The Library,** a casual oasis where guests enjoy everything from breakfast to late night supper. Gidaly attended SUNY at Albany, New York, and the University of Montpellier in France, is a member of the James Beard Foundation and is a Gold Medal Winner of the Société Culinaire Philanthropique of New York.

On Manhattan's exclusive Upper East Side, THE REGENCY HOTEL is known for exceptional service and understated elegance. Each of the 362 rooms and suites provides a residential atmosphere of comfort and luxury, and its Park Avenue location is convenient to the world's best shopping, theaters, business, and cultural attractions. Renowned as the birthplace of the "power breakfast," the 540 PARK restaurant showcases uptown contemporary American cuisine. THE LIBRARY is a cozy retreat for light snacks, drinks, Afternoon Tea, late supper, or simply to unwind with a good book in one of the oversized sofas or chairs. There is also a 2,000-square foot FITNESS CENTER with sauna and steam room.

*The discovery of a new dish does more
for human happiness than the discovery of a new star.*
—*Brillat-Savarin*

3

LOBSTER COCKTAIL

Serves 6

1 cup crème fraîche

1½ teaspoons grated orange zest

1 teaspoon grated lemon zest

1 teaspoon fresh lime juice

1 teaspoon fresh orange juice

1 teaspoon chopped fresh tarragon

Salt and freshly ground black pepper

1 European hothouse cucumber (1 pound)

2 small Belgian endive

3 cups cooked lobster meat (18 to 20 ounces), cut into 1-inch pieces

12 fresh chive sprigs, for garnish

Mesclun, for garnish

In a medium bowl, combine crème fraîche, orange and lemon zest, lime and orange juice, and the tarragon. Add salt and pepper to taste. Cover with plastic wrap and refrigerate to infuse flavors.

Trim ends from cucumber. Thinly slice one-fourth of the cucumber until you have 30 slices. Halve and seed remaining cucumber and julienne. Place julienned cucumber in small bowl. Trim endive and remove 12 small spears for garnish; julienne remainder of endive and place in bowl with cucumber; cover with plastic wrap. Wrap cucumber slices and endive spears separately in plastic wrap and refrigerate until ready to assemble lobster cocktail.

Just before serving, mix ¾ cup of the crème fraîche sauce with the lobster meat. Mix remaining sauce with the julienned cucumber and endive.

To serve, line six martini glasses with overlapping cucumber slices. Divide cucumber-endive salad into each glass. Top with lobster salad. Tuck in 2 endive spears and place chives, cut to fit, in the inside curve of the endive spears. Sprinkle a few mesclun leaves over the lobster salad.

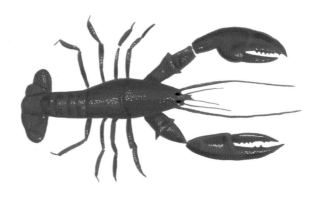

PAN-SEARED CHILI-CRUSTED RED SNAPPER
with OKRA TOMATO GUMBO

Preheat oven to 350°F.

Set aside 1 tablespoon chili powder. On waxed paper, combine remaining chili powder, ½ teaspoon of the salt and ¼ teaspoon of the pepper; mix with a fork to combine. Coat fillets with the chili mixture.

In a large, nonstick skillet, heat 3 tablespoons of the oil over medium-low heat. Pan-sear the fish in batches on both sides, being careful not to burn the fillets, about 1 minute. Transfer to a jelly-roll pan and bake 8-10 minutes or until fish flakes easily with a fork; keep warm.

Meanwhile, wipe out skillet. Add remaining oil and heat over medium-low heat. Add onions and garlic; sauté 3 minutes. Add okra, tomatoes, red and yellow peppers, oregano, reserved 1 tablespoon chili powder and remaining salt and pepper; sauté 3 minutes. Add chicken or shellfish stock and cook, uncovered, at a low boil until okra is crunchy-tender, about 10 minutes. Remove from heat; stir in lemon juice and filé powder.

To serve, place some rice in a shallow soup bowl; top with okra tomato gumbo and a fish fillet. Garnish with cilantro or parsley sprigs.

Serves 6

½ cup chili powder

1 teaspoon salt

½ teaspoon freshly ground black pepper

6 red snapper fillets (6 ounces each)

6 tablespoons olive oil

1 cup diced onion

4 garlic cloves, finely chopped

1 pound fresh okra, washed, trimmed and coarsely chopped (3 cups)

2 large tomatoes (8 ounces each), cored and diced

1 medium red bell pepper, seeded and finely chopped (1 cup)

1 medium yellow bell pepper, seeded and finely chopped (1 cup)

½ teaspoon dried oregano

1½ cups chicken stock, canned low-sodium chicken broth or shellfish stock

2 tablespoons fresh lemon juice

½ teaspoon filé powder

3 cups hot cooked rice

Cilantro or parsley sprigs for garnish

PEACH ᴀɴᴅ BLUEBERRY CRISP

Serves 6

¾ cup old-fashioned rolled oats, not quick-cooking

⅔ cup all-purpose flour

½ cup firmly packed light brown sugar

Pinch of salt

5 tablespoons unsalted butter, softened

8 large unpeeled ripe peaches (about 2½ pounds), halved, pitted and sliced (6 cups)

1 cup fresh blueberries

1 tablespoon fresh lemon juice

1 teaspoon vanilla

½ cup sugar

2 teaspoons cornstarch

½ teaspoon ground cinnamon

Pinch of ground allspice

Vanilla ice cream

Preheat oven to 325°F. Place six 10-ounce ramekins or custard cups on a jelly-roll pan; set aside.

In a medium bowl, combine oats, flour, brown sugar and salt. Work in butter with a fork or fingertips until mixture is crumbly; set aside.

In a large bowl, combine peaches, blueberries, lemon juice, vanilla, sugar, cornstarch, cinnamon and allspice; toss gently to mix. Spoon fruit into ramekins or custard cups. Sprinkle crumb mixture evenly over fruit. Bake 1 hour or until fruit is tender and topping is golden brown. Serve warm with ice cream.

Loews Coronado Bay Resort

San Diego, California

EXECUTIVE CHEF JAMES BOYCE

James Boyce's love affair with the kitchen dates to his first job at 14, making bagels in Poughkeepsie, New York. Now Chef Boyce puts his considerable talents to work in this resort's two popular eateries—**Azzura Point** and **RRR's American Cafe and Market**—blending Southern California's fresh produce and seafood with Mediterranean influences. A graduate of the Culinary Institute of America, Boyce worked with Daniel Boulud at New York's legendary Le Cirque and at such resorts as The Phoenician in Scottsdale, Arizona, and Caesars Palace in Las Vegas. His clear, modern style has won accolades from the Los Angeles Times and Travel & Leisure, and he was named one of America's three top seafood chefs by Simply Seafood magazine.

On a private 15-acre peninsula on San Diego's Coronado Bay, Loews Coronado Bay Resort features a variety of waterfront dining experiences, from award-winning gourmet cuisine to poolside snacks. From expansive bayfront windows, the acclaimed Azzura Point restaurant offers spectacular ocean views and a romantic ambience. RRR's American Cafe and Market provides outdoor all-day dining and picnics-to-go for beach or boat. Other amenities of this 440-room resort include a health club, tennis courts, three pools, a marina and private access to the beach.

And the fish were the brightest that e're flounced in nets.

—Lord Byron

CIDER-GLAZED APPLEWOOD SMOKED SALMON
WITH WATERCRESS AND ENDIVE SALAD

Serves 6

2-3 handfuls of apple, cherry or alder wood chips for the grill

¾ cup apple cider

2 tablespoons honey

¼ cup grainy mustard

2 tablespoons chopped fresh dill

¾ teaspoon grated fresh or prepared horseradish

1 2-pound side of salmon fillet, in one piece

Salt and sugar to taste

Watercress and Endive Salad (recipe follows)

Soak the wood chips in cold water for at least 30 minutes. Prepare a medium fire in a covered charcoal or gas grill. Just before cooking, toss the wet chips onto the coals or add to the gas grill according to the manufacturer's directions. Cut a piece of heavy cardboard to fit the size of the salmon. Wrap the cardboard completely with aluminum foil; set aside.

In a medium saucepan over high heat, reduce apple cider to ¼ cup, about 3-4 minutes. Stir in honey; cool. Fold in mustard, dill and horseradish.

Season both sides of the salmon with salt and a generous pinch of sugar. Place salmon, skin side down, on prepared cardboard. Brush salmon generously with part of the apple cider mixture. Place cardboard with the salmon on the grill; close cover and cook 15-20 minutes or until salmon flakes easily with a fork. Let salmon stand 10 minutes before cutting into serving portions. Salmon can be made a day ahead and chilled, if desired.

To serve, divide salad among 6 serving plates. Top with a piece of salmon and a spoonful of the apple cider mixture.

WATERCRESS AND ENDIVE SALAD

Serves 6

1 large bunch watercress, trimmed of thick stems

1 Belgian endive (3 ounces), trimmed and julienned (1 cup) [see NOTE]

¾ cup peeled and julienned daikon radish

¾ cup peeled and julienned carrot

3 tablespoons olive oil

1 tablespoon fresh lemon juice

Salt and cracked white pepper

In a large bowl, combine watercress, endive, radish and carrot. In a small bowl, whisk together oil and lemon. Add salt and pepper to taste. Add vinaigrette to the salad just before serving; toss.

NOTE: A mandoline or vegetable slicer with a julienne blade makes preparing the vegetables easier.

GRILLED HALIBUT
WITH HERB AND GARLIC-ROASTED NEW POTATOES AND SUMMER TOMATO-ORANGE RELISH

Prepare a medium-high fire in a covered charcoal or gas grill.

In a large bowl, place potatoes, garlic, 2 tablespoons of the oil and the herb sprigs. Sprinkle with salt and pepper to taste and toss to coat. Tear off a large sheet of heavy-duty aluminum foil. Place potato mixture in center of foil, then fold the sides up to enclose the potatoes in a pouch. Set pouch over hot grill and roast 15-20 minutes or until potatoes are tender. Move pouch to outer edge of grill to keep warm.

While potatoes are roasting, bring a saucepan of water to a boil. Fill a bowl with ice and water. Cut a small "X" on the bottom of each tomato. Plunge tomatoes into boiling water for 30 seconds or until tomato skin begins to split. Immediately plunge into ice water to cool. Drain tomatoes; core, peel, quarter and seed. Dice tomatoes and place in a medium bowl. Add remaining oil, vinegar and orange juice; mix gently to combine. Add salt and pepper to taste.

Season halibut with salt and pepper. Oil the grill rack. Place the fish, skin side up, on the grill. Grill, turning once with a wide spatula, until the fish flakes easily when tested with a fork, 10-14 minutes total.

To serve, arrange roasted potatoes and garlic in a small pile on each serving plate. Top with fish. Spoon the tomato-orange relish around the fish using a slotted spoon. Garnish with orange segments and herb sprigs.

Serves 4

1½ pounds small red potatoes (6 to 8), scrubbed and quartered

1 small head garlic, papery outer skin removed, quartered

⅓ cup olive oil

1 sprig fresh thyme, plus some for garnish

1 sprig fresh rosemary, plus some for garnish

Salt and freshly ground black pepper

2 medium, ripe red tomatoes

2 medium, ripe yellow tomatoes

¼ cup sherry vinegar

2 tablespoons freshly squeezed orange juice

4 halibut or sea bass fillets (6 ounces each)

Orange segments for garnish

LEMON CURD TART

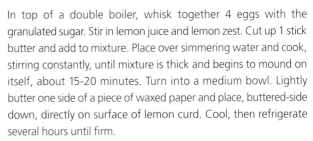

Serves 8

5	large eggs, at room temperature
1¼	cups granulated sugar
6	tablespoons fresh lemon juice
2	tablespoons grated lemon zest
1	cup (2 sticks) unsalted butter
1½	cups all-purpose flour
¼	cup confectioners sugar
¼	teaspoon salt

In top of a double boiler, whisk together 4 eggs with the granulated sugar. Stir in lemon juice and lemon zest. Cut up 1 stick butter and add to mixture. Place over simmering water and cook, stirring constantly, until mixture is thick and begins to mound on itself, about 15-20 minutes. Turn into a medium bowl. Lightly butter one side of a piece of waxed paper and place, buttered-side down, directly on surface of lemon curd. Cool, then refrigerate several hours until firm.

In a small bowl, beat remaining egg slightly. Cut remaining 1 stick butter into small pieces. In food processor bowl, combine flour, confectioners sugar and salt; pulse once or twice. Add butter and pulse until mixture resembles coarse crumbs. Turn into a large bowl, add beaten egg and combine with a fork until mixture is moistened. Gather into a ball and flatten into a disk. Cover with plastic wrap and chill at least 30 minutes.

Roll pastry out on a lightly floured surface to a 12-inch round. Fold dough in half and place in a 9-inch tart pan with removable bottom. Unfold pastry and ease into pan, gently pressing lightly over bottom and up sides of pan. Trim pastry to ¼ inch and fold edge inside to make an even, rounded rim of pastry. Prick bottom of pastry with tines of a fork. Chill at least 15 minutes.

Meanwhile, preheat oven to 375°F.

Place a piece of foil over the pastry. Fill the pan with pie weights, raw rice or dried beans. Bake 25 minutes, then remove the foil and weights and bake 5 minutes longer or until lightly browned. Cool completely on a wire rack.

Fill cooled pastry with the chilled lemon curd and refrigerate until ready to serve.

A Menu for Fall

Smoked Salmon
with Corn Cakes

Turkey Breast Stuffed
with Wild Mushrooms and
Virginia Ham

Mashed Sweet Potatoes
with Chestnuts

Caramelized Brussels Sprouts
and Red Onions

Cranberry Cilantro Relish
(page 20)

Watercress and Endive Salad
(page 8)

Pear Crisp with
Schnapps Ice Cream

SMOKED SALMON WITH CORN CAKES

Serves 6

¾ cup all-purpose flour

¾ cup coarse cornmeal (polenta)

1 teaspoon salt

1 teaspoon sugar

½ teaspoon baking powder

½ teaspoon baking soda

1¼ cups buttermilk

2 tablespoons unsalted butter, melted

1 large egg, lightly beaten

1 cup fresh corn kernels or vacuum-packed, drained

¼ cup finely chopped scallions

1 cup crème fraîche

1½ tablespoons prepared white horseradish, drained

2 tablespoons chopped fresh dill plus sprigs for garnish

¾ pound smoked salmon, thinly sliced

In a large bowl, combine flour, cornmeal, salt, sugar, baking powder and baking soda; stir to combine. In a medium bowl, whisk together buttermilk and melted butter. Whisk in egg. Add all at once to dry ingredients and blend just to combine.

In food processor, puree ½ cup corn until consistency of cooked oatmeal. Fold into batter with the remaining corn and the scallions. If batter is thick, thin with additional buttermilk, a tablespoon at a time. The mixture should have the consistency of a pancake batter. Let stand at room temperature 30 minutes.

Heat a nonstick griddle over medium-low heat. Coat lightly with additional butter. For each corn cake, drop batter by one level measuring tablespoon onto hot griddle. Cook, 1½-2 minutes, or until corn cake is golden, turning once. Keep hot in a warm oven. Makes 36 2½-inch cakes.

In a small bowl, combine crème fraîche with horseradish and chopped dill.

To serve, drape equal amounts of smoked salmon onto serving plates. Arrange corn cakes around salmon. Serve with crème fraîche-dill sauce. Garnish with dill sprigs.

TURKEY BREAST STUFFED
WITH WILD MUSHROOMS AND
VIRGINIA HAM

Clean mushrooms; remove and discard stems from Shiitakes and Portobellos. Roughly chop all the mushrooms.

In a large, deep nonstick skillet, or two smaller skillets [if using 2 skillets, divide the following ingredients evenly between them], heat oil over high heat; add ham and cook 1 minute. Add mushrooms and shallots; sauté 10-12 minutes or until liquid is absorbed and mushrooms start to stick to the bottom of the skillet. Transfer to a large bowl. Add thyme, 1 teaspoon salt and the pepper; cool. Cover with plastic wrap and refrigerate until cold, about 1 hour.

Preheat oven to 500°F.

Add ground turkey, eggs, and remaining 1 teaspoon salt to cooled mushroom mixture, mix thoroughly.

Place turkey breast, skin-side down, on work surface. Spread mushroom mixture over the turkey breast, leaving a 2-inch border on all sides. Bring top and bottom edges up over the filling [use wooden picks to hold in place, if necessary]; fold one side over the filling and then bring skin-side over to enclose. Slide butchers' twine under the turkey roll and tie loosely at 2-inch intervals, being careful not to tie too tightly or filling will ooze out. Slide twine lengthwise under roast and then loop under each knot on top; tie ends. You should have a roast about 12 inches long and about 4½ inches wide. Remove wooden picks, if used.

Carefully turn roast over, skin-side up, and place in roasting pan. Brush lightly with oil and season with salt and pepper. Roast 20 minutes or until well-browned. Reduce oven temperature to 325°F. Continue to roast 1-1½ hours or until internal temperature registers 165°F. and breast meat registers 170°F. on an instant-read thermometer. Let rest 10-15 minutes. Remove twine and cut into ½-inch slices.

Serves 8

¼   pound Shiitake mushrooms

¼   pound Portobello mushrooms

¼   pound Oyster mushrooms

¼   pound Crimini mushrooms

¼   cup vegetable oil, plus some for brushing over turkey

2   ounces minced Virginia ham (1 cup)

¾   cup minced shallots

1   tablespoon chopped fresh thyme

2   teaspoons salt

¼   teaspoon freshly ground black pepper

1   pound lean ground turkey

2   large eggs, lightly beaten

1   boneless turkey breast with skin on (2¾ to 3 pounds), butterflied and pounded ½-inch thick [have the butcher do this]

    Butchers' twine or heavy kitchen string

MASHED SWEET POTATOES
WITH CHESTNUTS

Serves 6 to 8

3 large sweet potatoes (1 pound each)

¼ cup milk

¼ cup (½ stick) unsalted butter, softened

1 cup chopped vacuum-packed or drained water-packed chestnuts

   Salt and freshly ground black pepper

Peel potatoes, quarter lengthwise then cut crosswise into 1-inch chunks. Place potatoes in a large saucepan with ¼ inch water. Bring to a boil over high heat. Reduce heat, cover and steam at a low boil 10-12 minutes or until potatoes are tender; drain. Return potatoes to saucepan and place over low heat a few minutes, shaking pan to dry potatoes. Remove from heat.

In small saucepan, heat milk and butter just until butter melts.

Beat potatoes with portable electric mixer or mash with potato masher until smooth. Add warmed milk mixture and beat until light and fluffy. Stir in chestnuts. Season to taste with salt and pepper.

CARAMELIZED BRUSSELS SPROUTS
AND RED ONIONS

Serves 6

2 containers (10 ounces each) fresh Brussels sprouts

1 package (10 ounces) unpeeled red pearl onions

2 tablespoons unsalted butter

   Salt and freshly ground black pepper

In a large saucepan, bring 1½ inches salted water to a boil. Remove wilted leaves from sprouts; trim off ends. Cut a small "X" into stem end of sprouts. Wash sprouts well; drain. Cook sprouts, covered, at a low boil 8 minutes or just until tender; drain and run under cold water to stop cooking. Drain again.

Meanwhile, in a medium saucepan, bring 1 inch salted water to a boil. Plunge unpeeled onions into water; bring back to boiling. Cook onions with cover slightly ajar at a low boil 4-6 minutes or just until tender; drain and rinse under cold water to stop cooking. With small, sharp knife, trim ends and slip off skins.

In a large skillet over moderately high heat, melt butter. When butter is foamy, add sprouts. **DO NOT STIR**. Let cook 3-4 minutes until caramelizing begins and sprouts start to brown; at this point, sprouts can be moved around. When lightly browned, add the onions. Cook and stir until vegetables are heated thoroughly. Add salt and pepper to taste.

PEAR CRISP
WITH SCHNAPPS ICE CREAM

Preheat oven to 375°F. Lightly butter an 8-inch square baking pan.

In a medium bowl, combine oats, flour, brown sugar and salt. Cut in butter with fingertips until crumbly, leaving some butter chunks.

Peel, halve, core and cut each pear half into 4 slices directly into a large bowl. Add lemon juice and toss gently to coat. Add honey, cornstarch and cinnamon; toss to combine. Place pears in prepared pan. Sprinkle evenly with crumb mixture.

Bake 25-35 minutes or until fruit is tender and topping is golden. Serve warm with Schnapps Ice Cream or whipped cream.

Serves 6 to 8

1	cup old-fashioned rolled oats, not quick cooking
1/2	cup all-purpose flour
1/2	cup firmly packed light brown sugar
1/8	teaspoon salt
1/2	cup (1 stick) unsalted butter, slightly softened but still cold
6	large firm-ripe pears, such as Bosc or Bartlett (2 1/2 pounds)
2	teaspoons fresh lemon juice
3	tablespoons honey
1	teaspoon cornstarch
1	teaspoon ground cinnamon
	Schnapps Ice Cream (recipe follows) or whipped cream

SCHNAPPS ICE CREAM

In a medium-size saucepan, heat milk over low heat until bubbles appear around edge of the pan.

Meanwhile, in a large bowl, lightly whisk together egg yolks with sugar. Gradually whisk in half of the scalded milk. Pour back into remaining milk in saucepan, blending well. Cook over low heat 5 minutes, stirring constantly until mixture thinly coats a metal spoon (160°F. on an instant-read thermometer). Do not allow mixture to come to a boil or it will curdle. Pour mixture into a medium-size bowl and set in a larger bowl filled with ice and water to cool custard and to stop the cooking, stirring occasionally. Stir in heavy cream. Cover with plastic wrap and chill several hours or overnight.

To freeze, stir in schnapps; place mixture in ice cream maker and freeze following manufacturer's directions. Spoon into plastic container and allow to mellow at least 2 hours in freezer.

Makes 1 quart

2	cups milk
6	large egg yolks, at room temperature
3/4	cup sugar
1	cup heavy cream
1/4	cup schnapps or good-quality whiskey

Loews Vanderbilt Plaza Hotel

Nashville, Tennessee

CHEF JOSH WEEKLEY

Chef Weekley grew up in south Florida and began his restaurant career at 17. After attending restaurant management college for two years, he graduated from the Culinary Institute of America and polished his skills in restaurants and catering operations in Ohio before heading for New York City, where he spent three years at the acclaimed Le Bernardin as Chef Tournant and Saucier. Active in many community and charitable organizations, Weekley is Chairman for Share Our Strength's "Taste of the Nation." He is also a committee member of Nashville's Wine Auction for the American Cancer Society, and of Star Chefs, which benefits the March of Dimes. Personal pleasures are also food-related— fishing and tending his own gardens.

In Nashville, "Music City U.S.A.," Loews Vanderbilt Plaza Hotel offers elegance and superb convenience to the city's cultural, business, medical, and educational centers. Its 338 luxury guest rooms include 12 suites, two concierge floors and an Executive Business Center. Meeting facilities can accommodate 12 to 1,200. In keeping with America's trend toward lighter, simpler fare, the Plaza Grill features grilled dishes, salads, sandwiches, and pastas.

Laughter is brightest where food is best.
—Irish Proverb

MUSTARD-CRUSTED
TROUT SALAD

Serves 4

- 8 ounces mesclun (8 cups)
- ¼ cup 1-inch pieces fresh chives
- ¼ cup assorted fresh herbs such as small basil leaves, tarragon, dill, cilantro or chervil
- 4 boneless trout fillets (4 to 5 ounces each), skin on

  Salt and freshly ground black pepper
- ¼ cup Dijon mustard
- ¾-1 cup fresh bread crumbs, preferably brioche
- 2 tablespoons olive oil

  Herbed Vinaigrette (recipe follows)
- 2 ripe yellow tomatoes, cored and thinly sliced
- 2 ripe red tomatoes, cored and thinly sliced

  Preserved Lemons [see **NOTE**]

In a large bowl, combine mesclun, chives and herbs; cover and refrigerate.

Rinse and dry the fillets with paper towels. Sprinkle with salt and pepper. Spread flesh side evenly with mustard; then coat generously with brioche crumbs.

In a large nonstick skillet, heat 1 tablespoon oil over low heat until faint ripples appear. Place 2 trout fillets, crumb-side down, in skillet. Cook over low heat until crumbs are golden brown, about 1½ minutes, shaking pan to prevent fish from sticking. Watch carefully to prevent crumbs from burning. Turn fillets carefully with a wide spatula; cook 2-3 minutes longer or until fish flakes easily with a fork. Transfer to a platter; cover and keep warm. Repeat with remaining tablespoon oil and trout fillets.

Remove mesclun from refrigerator. Drizzle with 2 to 4 tablespoons of the Herbed Vinaigrette; toss to coat. Place greens in center of large serving plates, dividing evenly. Arrange 2 slices each of yellow and red tomatoes around greens in a circle. Place a trout fillet on top of greens. Garnish with a preserved lemon wedge.

NOTE: Preserved lemons can be found in shops that stock Middle Eastern products.

HERBED VINAIGRETTE

Makes about 1 cup

- ¼ cup olive oil
- ¼ cup vegetable oil
- 1 tablespoon walnut oil
- 2 tablespoons sherry vinegar
- 2 tablespoons red wine vinegar
- 1 teaspoon Dijon mustard
- 2 tablespoons finely chopped fresh herbs [see **NOTE**]

  Salt and freshly ground black pepper

In a glass measure, combine olive, vegetable and walnut oils. In a small bowl, whisk together sherry vinegar, red wine vinegar and mustard. Gradually whisk in oils. Stir in herbs. Taste for salt and pepper.

NOTE: Select mild and stronger flavored herbs in combination, using no more than three herbs such as chives, basil, tarragon, dill, cilantro or chervil.

SMOKED DUCK BREAST with
CRANBERRY CILANTRO RELISH

Make Cranberry Cilantro Relish and refrigerate.

In a medium bowl, combine sugar, salt, coriander seed and white pepper. With a small sharp knife, score duck skin 2 to 3 times in a criss-cross pattern down the length of each duck breast. Generously coat the breasts, on both sides, with the sugar/spice mixture, patting on mixture firmly. Place in a shallow dish large enough to hold duck breasts in a single layer. Pour over any remaining sugar/spice mixture. Cover and refrigerate for three hours.

Prepare the smoker according to manufacturer's directions. Soak wood chips in cold water at least 30 minutes, then add to the smoker.*

Rinse duck breasts thoroughly to remove curing ingredients; pat completely dry with paper towels. Place breasts, skin-side up, in smoker and smoke approximately 2 hours, turning once, until internal temperature registers 160°F.-165°F. on an instant-read thermometer. Remove breasts from smoker and let rest on a plate 10-15 minutes. Remove duck skin and discard. Cover plate with plastic wrap and refrigerate 2-3 hours.

To serve, slice duck breasts thinly on a diagonal, keeping each duck breast separate. Spoon some Cranberry Cilantro Relish in center of each plate and fan duck breast slices around relish. Garnish with cilantro sprigs.

*If smoker is not available, use an old baking pan and place on coals of a covered grill. When pan gets very hot, place prepared wood chips in pan and close grill lid. When smoke begins to develop, place breasts on grill, close lid and smoke to required temperature.

NOTE: Ready-prepared smoked duck breasts can be purchased at specialty food shops or by mail order.

Serves 4

Cranberry Cilantro Relish (recipe follows)

1   cup firmly packed light brown sugar

½   cup coarse (kosher) salt

1   tablespoon ground coriander seed

1   teaspoon white pepper

4   Muscovy or Long Island duck breast halves (6 to 7 ounces each) [see NOTE]

Apple or cherry wood chips

Cilantro sprigs for garnish

CRANBERRY CILANTRO RELISH

Makes 2 cups

1 large navel orange

2 tablespoons dried cranberries

2 tablespoons coarsely chopped toasted hazelnuts

2 tablespoons chopped fresh cilantro

1 tablespoon seeded and minced poblano chili

1 1/2 cups fresh cranberries (1/2 of a 12-ounce package)

1/2 cup sugar

Using a small paring knife, remove the peel and white pith from the orange. Working over a bowl to catch juices, section orange and cut sections into small pieces. Add dried cranberries, hazelnuts, cilantro and poblano chili.

Place fresh cranberries in food processor and pulse until coarsely chopped. Add to ingredients in bowl with sugar; stir to combine. Cover with plastic wrap and refrigerate until ready to use.

BUTTERSCOTCH PECAN PIE

Serves 8

1 9-inch unbaked pie shell

3/4 cup sugar

3 tablespoons all-purpose flour

1/2 teaspoon salt

2 large eggs

1/2 cup evaporated milk

1 teaspoon vanilla

1 (12.25-ounce) jar fat-free butterscotch-flavored topping

2 tablespoons unsalted butter, melted

1 1/2 cups pecan halves

Prepare your favorite recipe for a single-crust 9-inch pie shell and refrigerate.

Preheat oven to 350°F.

In a large bowl, place sugar, flour and salt. Stir with a whisk a few times to combine. Add eggs, evaporated milk and vanilla. Whisk together until smooth. Stir in butterscotch topping and melted butter until combined.

Spread pecan halves in bottom of unbaked pie shell. Gently pour in the butterscotch filling. The pecans will rise to the top. Bake 55-60 minutes or until golden and filling is set. Cool completely on a wire rack. Refrigerate at least 2 hours before serving.

Loews Ventana Canyon Resort

Tucson, Arizona

EXECUTIVE CHEF JIM MAKINSON

Chef Makinson leads the culinary team at this desert oasis where his creations can be tasted in the **Ventana Room,** the all-day **Canyon Cafe, Bill's Grill** poolside, the casual indoor/outdoor **Flying V Bar & Grill,** the **Cascade Lounge** and the property's many banquet rooms. Makinson's experience includes positions as Executive Chef at the Kingsmill Resort, the Beverly Wilshire Hotel, The Boulders Resort, Kapalua Bay Hotel in Maui and the Maui Prince Hotel. This London-born chef has also done consulting work for The Regent Taiwan and trained in Tokyo with Sebu Hotels. Like many of his colleagues, Chef Makinson grows his own vegetables and considers basil and tomatoes to be his favorite ingredients.

Loews Ventana Canyon Resort, one of America's foremost resorts, nestles on 93 acres of Tucson's Catalina Mountain foothills and offers 366 rooms and 25 suites with terraces to capture the splendid beauty of the desert. The array of dining options ranges from the gourmet, award-winning Ventana Room, ranked first in Southwestern cuisine by *Condé Nast Traveler* Readers' Survey, to the informal Southwestern/Latin American food and panoramic views of two Fazio-designed PGA golf courses from the spacious patio of the Flying V Bar & Grill. Recreational amenities include tennis, croquet, a full-service spa and health club, hiking, two pools, and shopping.

Strange to see how a good dinner and feasting reconciles everybody.
—Samuel Pepys

WINTER SQUASH SOUP
WITH LITTLENECK CLAMS

Serves 12

- **2** tablespoons unsalted butter or olive oil
- **2²/₃** cups thinly sliced leeks, white part only
- **1/₃** cup finely chopped onion
- **2** butternut squash (1¹/₂ pounds each), peeled, halved, seeds removed and cut into 1-inch chunks (about 4 cups)
- **8** cups chicken stock or canned low-sodium chicken broth

  Salt and white pepper
- **2** dozen Littleneck clams, cleaned

In a large saucepot, melt butter or heat oil over medium-high heat. Add ³/₄ cup leeks and onions; sauté until tender, about 7-8 minutes. Add squash, remaining leeks and the chicken stock. Bring to a boil over medium-high heat; lower heat and simmer, covered, until squash is soft, about 15-20 minutes. Cool slightly. In food processor or blender, puree soup, in batches, until smooth and place in a large bowl. Return pureed soup to saucepot, add salt and pepper to taste and heat to serving temperature.

Meanwhile, in a large, wide pot, combine ¹/₂ cup water with the clams. Cover tightly and bring to a boil. Reduce heat and steam 5-10 minutes or until shells open. Discard any that do not open. Strain clam liquid and reserve for another use.

To serve, ladle soup into shallow bowls; garnish each serving with clams.

ROAST PHEASANT
WITH PORT WINE SAUCE, ROASTED SHALLOTS AND CREAMY PARSNIPS

Remove feet and any pin feathers from pheasants or have butcher do this for you. Rinse inside and out under cold running water and pat dry with paper towels. Use 1 tablespoon of the olive oil to rub skin of pheasants. Season with salt and pepper. Combine garlic, thyme and rosemary in a small cup; rub mixture over birds. Fold wings and tie legs together with twine to maintain shape.

Preheat oven to 350°F.

Heat the remaining 2 tablespoons oil in a large, heavy pan set over two burners on top of stove. Brown pheasants on all sides. Turn each pheasant on its side, leg down, and place in oven. Roast 15 minutes then turn to other side, leg down, and roast 15 minutes longer. Turn breast-side up and roast 35-45 minutes until the internal temperature registers 160°F. on an instant-read thermometer inserted into the drumstick near, but not touching, the leg bone. Baste pheasants occasionally during roasting. Remove pheasants to a platter and tent with foil to keep warm.

While pheasants are roasting, prepare Roasted Shallots and Creamy Parsnips.

Drain off fat from roasting pan into a glass measure or fat separator. Return 2 tablespoons fat to the drippings in the roasting pan and set on top of stove. Add slivered shallots and sauté until soft, but not brown. Add wine and port and bring to a boil over high heat, stirring to scrape up browned bits in pan. Cook and stir 5-7 minutes until mixture is reduced by half and begins to look syrupy. Gradually stir in butter in small bits. Strain into a sauce boat; keep warm.

To serve, remove twine from birds and cut each in half, removing backbone. Place Creamy Parsnips on serving plates. Place half a pheasant on top. Spoon over some of the Port Wine Sauce and garnish with Roasted Shallots.

Serves 4

- 2 young pheasants (2½ to 3 pounds each)
- 3 tablespoons olive oil
- 2 teaspoons salt
- 2 teaspoons freshly ground black pepper
- 2 tablespoons minced fresh garlic (paste-like consistency)
- 2 tablespoons finely chopped fresh thyme
- 1 tablespoon finely chopped fresh rosemary

Roasted Shallots (recipe follows)

Creamy Parsnips (recipe follows)

- ½ cup slivered shallots
- 1 cup dry red wine
- ¼ cup ruby port
- 2 tablespoons unsalted butter

ROASTED SHALLOTS

Cooking the shallots in milk draws out any strong onion flavor.

Makes 6 garnishes

6   large shallots, peeled
2   cups milk
1   tablespoon unsalted butter

In a small saucepan, combine shallots with milk. Heat slowly to a boil, drain in a mesh strainer and rinse shallots under cold running water to stop cooking. Pat shallots dry with paper towels.

In a medium skillet over low heat, melt butter. Add shallots and turn to coat with butter. Sauté shallots until golden brown, about 12-15 minutes, turning frequently. Keep warm.

CREAMY PARSNIPS

Serves 4 to 6

2   pounds parsnips
2   tablespoons fresh lemon juice
½   cup heavy cream
¼   cup (½ stick) unsalted butter
    Salt and white pepper

Peel and halve parsnips lengthwise (quarter, if large). Cut into ½-inch pieces. Cook parsnips, covered, in 1 inch boiling salted water with the lemon juice until tender, about 15 minutes; drain.

In a small saucepan, heat cream with butter just until butter is melted. Place parsnips in food processor. Process, in pulses, for a few seconds. Through feeder tube, add warmed cream mixture, processing in pulses, until creamy smooth. Add salt and white pepper to taste.

TEQUILA LIME SORBET

In a small saucepan, combine sugar and water. Cook and stir over medium-low heat until sugar dissolves. Remove from heat and cool to room temperature.

In a medium bowl, combine the sugar syrup, lime juice and tequila; cover and refrigerate until very cold, about 3 hours. Pour mixture into canister of an ice cream maker and freeze according to manufacturer's directions. Or pour mixture into a 9-inch square metal pan and freeze until solid, about 6 hours, stirring occasionally to bring firm edges of the tequila sorbet into the soft center; break into chunks and process until smooth in a food processor. Spoon into plastic container and refreeze until firm.

Makes 3½ cups

- 1½ cups sugar
- 1½ cups water
- 1 cup fresh lime juice
- 2 tablespoons tequila

MEXICAN WEDDING CAKES

Preheat oven to 350°F.

In a large bowl, with electric mixer at medium-high speed, beat butter, ½ cup confectioners sugar and vanilla until fluffy and light. With mixer at medium-low speed, gradually add the flour, beating until the mixture forms a dough. Stir in pecans. Place remaining confectioners sugar in a pie plate and reserve.

Using 1 level measuring tablespoon at a time, roll dough between palms of hands. Place 1 inch apart on large ungreased cookie sheets and flatten slightly with fingers.

Bake 15-18 minutes or just until the cookies begin to turn golden. Cool slightly on baking sheets set on wire racks. Roll hot cookies, a few at a time, in reserved confectioners sugar to coat (turning between two forks helps). Place the coated cookies on wire racks to cool completely.

Makes 3 dozen

- 1 cup (2 sticks) unsalted butter, softened
- 1½ cups confectioners sugar
- 1 teaspoon vanilla
- 2 cups sifted bread flour
- 1 cup finely chopped pecans

Loews Annapolis Hotel
Annapolis, Maryland

EXECUTIVE CHEF JOHN ROCCA

Chef Rocca oversees all aspects of food and beverage for this Chesapeake Bay hotel, including the **Corinthian Restaurant**, reminiscent of formal dining rooms in historic Maryland houses. A favorite among Maryland State Delegates, the Corinthian has also received the Award of Excellence from Wine Spectator magazine. And, while the menu boasts some of the region's most prized specialties—Maryland Crab Cakes, of course—Chef Rocca is also the proud recipient of the Baltimore on Ice Award, which recognized his expertise in ice carving. Along with gardening, Rocca enjoys water skiing, and building and flying model airplanes.

In this charming corner of colonial America, along the shores of Chesapeake Bay, Loews Annapolis Hotel is the largest and most luxurious hotel in Maryland's capital city. Approached by a secluded courtyard, the handsome red-brick hotel offers 217 superbly comfortable guest rooms, more than 16,000 square feet of meeting and function space and a self-contained Powerhouse with 4,140 square feet of flexible space. One of the premier restaurants in the region, the hotel's Corinthian is complemented by The Weather Rail Lounge and Sports Bar, a popular destination for light fare and evening entertainment.

No man can be wise on an empty stomach.
—George Eliot

27

MARYLAND CRAB CAKES
WITH MARINATED TOMATOES AND LEMON AÏOLI

Serves 6 as an appetizer or
4 as a main course

¼ cup mayonnaise

1 large egg, lightly beaten

1 teaspoon Old Bay seafood seasoning

1 teaspoon dry mustard

¼ teaspoon Worcestershire sauce

1 pound jumbo lump crabmeat, drained and picked over to remove shells and cartilage

1½ cups fresh bread crumbs, crusts removed

2 tomatoes, cut in wedges

1½ tablespoons unsalted butter

1½ tablespoons vegetable oil

Lemon Aïoli (recipe follows)

In a large bowl, combine mayonnaise, egg, seafood seasoning, dry mustard and Worcestershire. Add crabmeat; mix lightly to combine. Blend in bread crumbs. Divide the crab mixture into 6 or 4 portions, depending on whether for an appetizer or main course, and shape into patties. Place on a plate, cover and chill 1½ hours to firm. Meanwhile, prepare Lemon Aïoli and Marinated Tomatoes made by adding Herbed Vinaigrette (page 18)—using small basil leaves instead of mixed herbs—to wedges of 2 ripe tomatoes. Cover and refrigerate at least 1 hour for flavors to mellow.

In a large skillet over medium heat, melt the butter with the oil. Fry the crab cakes until lightly browned on both sides, about 7-9 minutes, turning carefully with a wide spatula. Serve with Marinated Tomatoes and Lemon Aïoli.

LEMON AÏOLI

Makes about 1 cup

2 garlic cloves, peeled and mashed into a paste

2 tablespoons fresh lemon juice

1 cup mayonnaise

Salt and white pepper

In a bowl, whisk together garlic paste, lemon juice and mayonnaise. Add salt and white pepper to taste. Cover and chill at least 1 hour for flavors to blend.

ROASTED STUFFED CAPON
with SAGE BUTTER and
CIDER GRAVY

In a large skillet, cook 5 slices bacon (¼ pound) until brown and crisp; drain on paper towels. Meanwhile, cut remaining bacon into ½-inch wide pieces and cook until brown and crisp; remove with a slotted spoon to paper towels. Set aside bacon pieces and ¼ cup of the bacon drippings for Herbed Oyster Stuffing.

In a small bowl, finely crumble the 5 bacon slices. Add softened butter and chopped sage; blend together with a wooden spoon. Set the sage/bacon butter aside or cover and refrigerate until ready to use. Bring back to room temperature before using.

Prepare Herbed Oyster Stuffing and refrigerate.

Set oven rack in lower third of oven. Preheat oven to 425°F.

Remove giblets and neck from capon and reserve for making giblet stock for gravy. Rinse capon under cold running water and pat dry. Stuff neck cavity loosely with stuffing; close cavity and secure with a skewer. Fill body cavity loosely with stuffing; close with skewers. Tie legs together; fold wings under bird.

Rub the sage/bacon butter all over the bird. Place capon, breast-side up, on rack in shallow roasting pan. Roast 30 minutes. Reduce oven temperature to 325°F. and roast 2½-3 hours longer, basting every 20 minutes, until internal temperature registers 180°F. on an instant-read thermometer inserted into the thickest part of the thigh without touching bone.

Remove capon from oven and place on a serving platter. Tent loosely with foil and let rest 20 minutes while preparing Cider Gravy. Remove skewers and twine from capon. Garnish platter with fresh sage leaves. Serve with gravy and Cranberry Sauce with Tarragon and Port Wine (page 31).

Before storing leftovers, it is important to remove any remaining stuffing from capon and refrigerate bird and stuffing separately.

NOTE: Since the number of bacon slices varies in each package, you will need twice as many slices for the stuffing as for the sage/bacon butter.

Serves 12 plus leftovers

¾ pound sliced bacon, about 15 slices [see NOTE]

½ cup (1 stick) unsalted butter, softened

1½ tablespoons finely chopped fresh sage leaves or 1½ teaspoons dried

Herbed Oyster Stuffing (recipe follows)

12 to 14 pound capon, thawed if frozen

Cider Gravy (recipe follows)

Fresh sage leaves for garnish

HERBED OYSTER STUFFING

Makes 9 cups

1 loaf unsliced white bread (1 pound), cut into ¾-inch cubes

¼ cup reserved bacon drippings

2 cups finely chopped onion

1½ cups chopped celery

3 tablespoons minced fresh thyme leaves

1 tablespoon minced fresh sage leaves

1 tablespoon minced fresh garlic

⅔ cup finely chopped fresh parsley

Reserved cooked bacon pieces

18 fresh oysters, shucked, drained and coarsely chopped

½ cup (1 stick) unsalted butter, melted

½ cup chicken stock or canned low-sodium chicken broth

Salt and freshly ground black pepper

Preheat oven to 325°F.

Place bread cubes on two jelly-roll pans in a single layer. Toast until dry and lightly golden, about 15 minutes. Turn into a large bowl.

In a large skillet over medium-high heat, heat the reserved bacon drippings. Add onion, celery, thyme, sage and garlic; sauté until tender, about 10 minutes. Add to bread cubes with parsley, the reserved cooked bacon pieces, oysters and the melted butter; mix lightly to combine. Add chicken broth; mix to moisten. Add salt and pepper to taste. Refrigerate until ready to use.

CIDER GRAVY

In a medium saucepan, combine capon neck, giblets (except liver), onion, carrot, celery tops, parsley sprigs, peppercorns and water. Heat to a boil; lower heat. Cover and simmer 1 hour; add liver and simmer 20 minutes longer.

Strain broth and measure. You should have 2 cups. Add water, if necessary. Discard neck, giblets and vegetables.

After capon is removed from roasting pan, tilt pan and drain off fat and pan juices into a glass measure or fat separator. Return ¼ cup fat to roasting pan, discard remaining fat but reserve pan juices in bottom of measure.

Whisk 6 tablespoons flour into roasting pan set over two burners on top of stove. Stir over low heat until mixture becomes golden and bubbly. Add cider, sherry, giblet stock and reserved pan juices; stir and scrape until all browned bits are dissolved. Cook, stirring constantly, until gravy thickens and bubbles. Simmer 5 minutes. Add salt and pepper to taste.

For a thicker gravy, place remaining 2 tablespoons flour in a small bowl and whisk in some of the hot gravy until smooth; then gradually pour mixture back into roasting pan and cook a few minutes longer, whisking constantly, until thickened.

Makes about 4 cups

	Capon neck and giblets
1	medium onion, quartered
1	medium carrot, cut into large chunks
	Few celery tops
	Few parsley sprigs
12	whole peppercorns
2½	cups water
¼	cup fat from roasting pan
6-8	tablespoons all-purpose flour
1	cup apple cider
1	cup dry sherry
	Salt and freshly ground black pepper

CRANBERRY SAUCE
with TARRAGON and PORT WINE

In a 3-quart saucepan, combine cranberries, sugar, port, lemon juice and orange zest. Bring to a boil over high heat. Reduce heat and simmer, uncovered, at a low boil, stirring occasionally, until the berries burst and mixture has thickened, about 15 minutes. Remove from heat and let cool to room temperature. Stir in tarragon. Transfer to a bowl, cover with plastic wrap and chill until very cold.

Makes 4 cups

1	package (12 ounces) fresh cranberries
1½	cups sugar
1	cup tawny port
2	tablespoons fresh lemon juice
1	teaspoon grated orange zest
3	tablespoons chopped fresh tarragon

BOURBON ICE CREAM

Makes 1 pint

½ cup bourbon

1 pint good-quality vanilla ice cream

In a heavy saucepan, bring bourbon to a boil. *Do not shake the pan.* Stand back as the bourbon may flame. If it does, wait a minute or two for the alcohol to burn off and the flame to subside. Reduce bourbon to ¼ cup, about 3-6 minutes. Remove from heat and cool to room temperature.

Soften the ice cream, but do not let it melt. Turn into a medium bowl. With a hand-held mixer or heavy whisk, combine bourbon with ice cream and refreeze until firm.

CHOCOLATE ESPRESSO COOKIES

Makes about 45 cookies

3 1-ounce squares unsweetened chocolate, coarsely chopped

2 cups (12 ounces) semi-sweet chocolate chips

½ cup (1 stick) unsalted butter, cut into pieces

1 tablespoon espresso coffee powder

¾ cup all-purpose flour, sifted after measuring

¼ teaspoon baking powder

¼ teaspoon salt

3 large eggs

1 cup plus 2 tablespoons sugar

1 cup coarsely chopped walnuts

Preheat oven to 350°F. Grease 2 large baking sheets.

In a heavy, medium saucepan, melt unsweetened chocolate, 1 cup of the chocolate chips and the butter over low heat; stir to combine. Remove from heat. Stir in coffee powder and cool.

On waxed paper, combine flour, baking powder and salt; set aside. In a large bowl with electric mixer on high speed, beat eggs until foamy, add sugar gradually and beat until mixture forms a ribbon when beaters are lifted, about 2-4 minutes. Reduce speed to low and gradually add the cooled chocolate mixture until combined. Blend in flour mixture. Stir in the remaining 1 cup chocolate chips and the walnuts.

Drop batter by heaping tablespoons, 2 inches apart on prepared baking sheets. Bake until cookies are set but still soft, 10-12 minutes. Cool on baking sheets 2 minutes then transfer to a wire rack; cool completely.

A Menu for Winter

Roasted Fennel
Tomato Bisque

Ale–Battered Shrimp
with Spicy Tartar Sauce and
Pilsner Slaw

Lamb Shanks with
White Beans, Sage and
Wild Mushrooms

Individual Pear and
Dried Cranberry Charlottes
with Custard Sauce

ROASTED FENNEL
TOMATO BISQUE

Serves 8

1   medium fennel bulb (about 1¼ pounds), stems and fronds removed, reserving some fronds for garnish

2   large carrots (½ pound), peeled, cut in half lengthwise and then into ½-inch pieces

1   large onion (8 ounces), peeled and cut into 1-inch dice

3   shallots, peeled and halved

4   large garlic cloves, peeled and lightly crushed

¼   cup olive oil

1   can (28 ounces) whole peeled tomatoes

2   tablespoons tomato paste

4   cups chicken stock or canned low-sodium chicken broth

1   cup heavy cream

1   teaspoon sugar, optional

1   teaspoon salt

¼   teaspoon white pepper

Preheat oven to 400°F.

Roughly chop fennel and combine with carrots, onion, shallots and garlic in a large bowl; add oil and toss to coat. Spread vegetables out on a jelly-roll pan and roast in oven until lightly browned, about 1 hour, turning once.

Place vegetables in a large, heavy-bottomed saucepot. Add whole peeled tomatoes, breaking up tomatoes against side of saucepot, tomato paste and chicken broth. Bring to a boil over high heat. Reduce heat and simmer, uncovered, 1 hour. Cool slightly.

In a food processor, puree soup, in batches, as smooth as possible, transferring batches to a large bowl. Set a wide, fine-mesh strainer over another bowl and add pureed mixture in batches, pressing soup and vegetables against side of strainer with a rubber spatula forcing mixture through. You should have 7 cups soup.

Pour soup back into saucepot. Blend in cream, sugar (if needed to balance acidity) salt and pepper. Heat over low heat to serving temperature; garnish with fennel fronds.

ALE-BATTERED SHRIMP
WITH SPICY TARTAR SAUCE AND
PILSNER SLAW

Prepare Spicy Tartar Sauce and Pilsner Slaw and refrigerate.

In a medium bowl, lightly whisk together the ale, water, eggs, rice flour, lemon pepper and paprika just until smooth. If mixture seems too thick, stir in 1 to 2 additional teaspoons ale.

In a large bowl, combine shrimp with the sesame oil, lemon juice, salt and pepper.

Pour vegetable oil to a 1-inch depth into a large, heavy, deep skillet or wide saucepan. Heat oil to 375°F. on a deep-fat frying thermometer. Line a large baking sheet with several thicknesses of paper towels. Preheat oven to 200°F.

Dip shrimp, one at a time, into the batter, holding by the tail and letting excess batter drip back into the bowl. With tongs, carefully lower shrimp into the hot oil; hold for 10 seconds then release into the oil. Fry, a few at a time, until lightly brown on bottom, about 40 seconds. Turn over and fry 1½-2 minutes until brown. Drain on paper towels. Keep warm in oven while frying remaining shrimp. Bring oil back to frying temperature before frying each batch.

To serve, arrange shrimp on a platter with tails in the air. Serve with bowls of Pilsner Slaw and Spicy Tartar Sauce on the side. Garnish with lemon wedges and accompany with your favorite beer.

NOTE: Rice flour is available in specialty food stores or the oriental food sections of many supermarkets.

Serves 6 to 8

Spicy Tartar Sauce (recipe follows)

Pilsner Slaw (recipe follows)

¾ cup amber ale

¼ cup ice water

2 large eggs

2 cups rice flour [see NOTE]

1 teaspoon lemon pepper seasoning

½ teaspoon paprika

2 pounds jumbo shrimp, peeled, deveined, butterflied with tail left on

¼ cup sesame oil

¼ cup fresh lemon juice

Salt and freshly ground black pepper

Vegetable oil for frying

Lemon wedges

SPICY TARTAR SAUCE

Makes 2 cups

1 cup mayonnaise

½ cup sour cream

⅓ cup roughly chopped garlic pickle

⅓ cup drained capers, roughly chopped

1 large hard-cooked egg, roughly chopped

1 tablespoon fresh lemon juice

1 teaspoon hot pepper sauce, such as Tabasco

¼ teaspoon cayenne pepper

In a medium bowl, blend together mayonnaise and sour cream. Stir in remaining ingredients. Cover and chill in refrigerator to mellow flavors.

PILSNER SLAW

Makes 8 cups

8 cups shredded cabbage

1 cup coarsely shredded carrot

1 cup seeded and diced red bell pepper

1 cup seeded and diced green bell pepper

¼ cup sugar

¼ cup Pilsner beer

¼ cup olive oil

1 tablespoon fresh lemon juice

1 teaspoon mustard seeds

Salt and freshly ground black pepper

In a large bowl, combine cabbage, carrots, and the red and green peppers.

In a small saucepan over low heat, warm sugar and beer, stirring constantly just until sugar is melted. Pour over vegetables. Add oil, lemon juice, mustard seeds, salt and pepper. Stir to combine. Cover with plastic wrap and chill several hours to mellow flavors.

LAMB SHANKS
with WHITE BEANS, SAGE and WILD MUSHROOMS

Place beans in a large saucepan and add enough water to cover the beans by 2 inches. Set uncovered over moderately-high heat and bring to a boil. Reduce heat and simmer beans at a low boil for 2 minutes. Turn off the heat, cover saucepan and let stand at room temperature 1 hour. Drain beans, discarding soaking liquid.

Meanwhile, wipe lamb shanks with dampened paper towels. Sprinkle shanks with salt and pepper and dredge with flour to coat. In a large, deep, heavy skillet or oval Dutch oven, heat oil over moderately-high heat until faint ripples appear. Add shanks, a few at a time, and brown well on all sides. Remove browned shanks with tongs to a bowl. You may have to add an additional tablespoon of oil to pan.

While shanks are browning, place oven rack in lower third of oven. Preheat oven to 350°F.

Add onions, carrots and garlic to pan. Sauté over medium heat until onions are translucent, about 5-7 minutes. Add sage and sauté 1 minute. Add cooled beans, wine and chicken broth; bring to a boil over high heat. If a skillet has been used for browning, transfer to a large roasting pan with a domed lid. Place lamb shanks on top, pushing down slightly into the beans. Cover and place pan in oven. Bake 1½-2 hours or until meat is tender.

Just before shanks are done, melt butter in a large skillet over medium-high heat. Add shallots and sauté 2 minutes. Add mushrooms, cook and stir until mushrooms are soft and liquid in pan has almost evaporated, about 5 minutes.

Remove roasting pan from oven and set shanks aside. Stir mushrooms into beans. Taste for salt and pepper.

To serve, divide bean mixture into large shallow soup bowls. Top with a lamb shank. Sprinkle with parsley if desired.

Serves 6

1	package (1 pound) dried white beans, such as Great Northern or navy
6	small lamb shanks (¾ to 1 pound each) cracked by butcher
	Salt and freshly ground black pepper
3-4	tablespoons all-purpose flour
3-4	tablespoons olive oil
2	cups chopped onion
½	cup diced carrots
6	large garlic cloves, minced
⅓	cup coarsely chopped fresh sage
1½	cups dry red wine
1¼	cups chicken stock or canned low-sodium chicken broth
2	tablespoons unsalted butter
¼	cup finely chopped shallots
6	ounces Chanterelle mushrooms, trimmed and cut into thin strips
6	ounces Shiitake mushrooms, trimmed and cut into thin strips
4	ounces Black Trumpet mushrooms
	Chopped fresh parsley, optional garnish

INDIVIDUAL PEAR
AND DRIED CRANBERRY CHARLOTTES WITH
CUSTARD SAUCE

Serves 8

Custard Sauce (recipe follows)

6 firm-ripe Red Bartlett pears (3 pounds), peeled, halved, cored and cut into 1/2-inch chunks

2/3 cup sugar

1 1/2 tablespoons fresh lemon juice

1 tablespoon water

1/2 cup dried cranberries

1/2 cup (1 stick) unsalted butter

23 slices firm thin-sliced white bread, preferably day-old

Mint sprigs for garnish

Prepare Custard Sauce and refrigerate.

In a large, deep skillet, combine pears with sugar, lemon juice and water. Bring to a boil over medium heat and cook, uncovered, stirring frequently, until pears are soft, about 10 minutes. Add cranberries and stir to combine. Remove from heat; cool.

Melt butter in a small skillet. Lightly brush insides of eight ramekins (3 x 1 1/2-inches) with butter, set aside.

Preheat oven to 350°F.

Trim crusts from bread slices. Using a 3-inch round cutter, cut out 16 rounds (use trimmings to make bread crumbs). Brush rounds and remaining bread slices on one side with melted butter. Place a bread round, butter-side down, in bottom of each ramekin. Cut each bread slice into 3 equal pieces, then crosswise into 9 equal squares. Line the sides of each ramekin with 7 of the bread squares, butter-side against the ramekin; trim off any bread that sticks above the rim. Completely fill the inside of each ramekin with about 1/3 cup of the pear mixture. Top each ramekin with one of the remaining bread rounds, butter-side up, and press down with heel of hand until bread round is about even with the rim of the ramekin. [It is important to compact the filling; otherwise, the charlottes will collapse when unmolded.] Set ramekins on a jelly-roll pan and bake 35-40 minutes or until bread is golden. Cool slightly.

To serve, loosen warm charlottes from ramekin with a small knife. Place dessert plate on top of ramekin and turn upside down; gently shake to loosen; remove ramekin. Spoon Custard Sauce around charlotte. Garnish with mint sprig. Serve warm.

CUSTARD SAUCE

Heat milk in top of double boiler set over direct heat until bubbles appear around edge of pan. In medium bowl, whisk together the egg yolks with sugar until creamy. Slowly pour hot milk into egg mixture, whisking constantly. Return to double boiler. Place over hot, not boiling, water (water in bottom of double boiler should not touch top part). Cook over low heat, stirring constantly, until a thin coating forms on a metal spoon, about 10 minutes. Immediately pour into a bowl. Set bowl in larger bowl filled with ice and water to stop cooking; stir occasionally. Remove from water bath, stir in vanilla and cinnamon. Cover with plastic wrap and chill several hours until very cold.

Makes 3 to 3¼ cups

2½   cups milk

6   large egg yolks

½   cup sugar

½   teaspoon vanilla

⅛   teaspoon ground cinnamon

LOEWS HOTEL VOGUE

Montréal, Canada

EXECUTIVE CHEF
ERIC FRAUDEAU

Eric Fraudeau's classical training and exposure to international influences give him a distinct culinary style. Born and raised in La Rochelle, France, he completed his apprenticeship in Michelin-starred establishments throughout France, including Le Pavillon des Boulevards in Bordeaux. His hotel career began at Hotel de Grace et Angleterre and eventually brought him to the Ritz Carlton group. After two years at Hotel Las Brisas in Acapulco, Fraudeau joined **Loews Hotel Vogue.** Along with his training, Chef Fraudeau's interest in cooking may also be genetic; his grandmother, his "inspiration," was a chef in a small auberge in France.

In the heart of Montréal's premier business and shopping districts, Loews Hotel Vogue combines the city's vitality and unique character with chic interiors, an intimate atmosphere, and uncompromising service. The hotel's 126 guest rooms and 16 suites feature oversized marble bathrooms with Jacuzzi and separate showers; 12 function rooms accommodate groups of eight to 240 people, and there is casually elegant dining in the Société Cafe and L'Opera Bar.

Serenely full, the epicure would say,
Fate cannot harm me, I have dined today.
—Sydney Smith

GREEN PEA SOUP
WITH CARDAMOM OIL DRIZZLE

Serves 8

½   teaspoon cardamom seeds, slightly crushed

¼   cup extra-virgin olive oil

1   package (1 pound) dry green split peas

8   cups chicken stock or canned low-sodium chicken broth

¼   cup fresh lemon juice

    Salt and white pepper

TWO DAYS BEFORE PREPARING SOUP, place cardamom and oil in a small skillet and slowly heat just until bubbles appear around the edge of the skillet. Transfer to a small bowl, cover and let stand at room temperature to infuse flavors.

To make soup, rinse peas under cold water in a colander. Place peas in a large saucepot with chicken stock or broth and bring to a boil; reduce heat, cover and simmer 1 hour or until peas are tender. Remove from heat and cool slightly.

Puree soup, in batches, in food processor or blender until smooth, transferring each batch to a bowl. Return pureed soup to saucepot, stir in lemon juice and heat to serving temperature. Add salt and white pepper to taste.

While soup is heating, strain cardamom oil into a small cup. Ladle soup into large soup bowls and drizzle each serving with some of the cardamom oil.

OSSO BUCCO WITH GARLIC PARMESAN
MASHED YELLOW POTATOES

Wipe osso bucco with dampened paper towel. Sprinkle with salt and pepper. Dredge with flour, shaking off excess.

Heat a large oval Dutch oven or heavy casserole over medium heat 5 minutes. Add oil and butter. Brown meat on all sides. Transfer to a bowl. Add onions, carrots, celery and garlic to pot; cook and stir until vegetables are a light golden brown, about 10-12 minutes. Add wine and bring to a boil; lower heat. Return osso bucco to Dutch oven or casserole. Cover and simmer 1½ hours or until meat is tender. Place in a bowl and cover with foil to keep warm.

Strain pan juices with vegetables into a large sieve set over a bowl; press vegetables with a rubber spatula to extract as much liquid as possible and to force some of them through the sieve. Return sauce to Dutch oven or casserole and add the vinegar. Bring to boiling over high heat and reduce to 1½ cups, about 10 minutes.

To serve, place some Garlic Parmesan Mashed Yellow Potatoes on serving plates. Top with osso bucco and spoon over the sauce. Garnish with parsley if desired.

NOTE: The chef uses venison for this dish. Venison can be purchased at specialty food shops or by mail order. If venison is not available, veal can be used.

Serves 6 to 8

8	pieces venison or veal osso bucco (8-10 ounces each), about 3 inches in diameter and 2 inches thick [see NOTE]
1	teaspoon salt
½	teaspoon freshly ground black pepper
¼	cup all-purpose flour
¼	cup vegetable oil
2	tablespoons unsalted butter
2	cups chopped onion
1	cup chopped carrots
½	cup chopped celery
8	garlic cloves, minced
3½	cups full-bodied red wine
1	tablespoon balsamic vinegar
	Garlic Parmesan Mashed Yellow Potatoes (recipe follows)
	Finely chopped parsley, optional

GARLIC PARMESAN MASHED
YELLOW POTATOES

Peel potatoes and cut into large chunks. Cook, covered, in 1 inch boiling salted water about 15-20 minutes or until fork tender, drain. Return to pan and heat 1 minute to dry potatoes.

In a small saucepan, warm cream, milk, butter and garlic until butter melts. In a large bowl, mash potatoes with a hand held mixer or potato masher. Gradually add warm cream mixture, beating constantly until potatoes are fluffy and creamy.

Stir in cheese.

Serves 6 to 8

8	large yellow potatoes, preferably Yukon Gold (3 pounds)
½	cup heavy cream
½	cup milk
¼	cup (½ stick) butter
½	teaspoon minced fresh garlic
½	cup freshly grated Parmigiano-Reggiano cheese

PEAR ᴀɴᴅ FIG TART
ᴡɪᴛʜ BLUE CHEESE AND PORT

Serves 4

- 1 cup ruby port
- ¾ cup firmly packed light brown sugar
- 1 frozen puff pastry sheet (from 17¼-ounce package), thawed according to package directions
- 4 small fresh purple figs
- 1 tablespoon fresh lemon juice
- 2 small, firm-ripe pears, such as Bosc or Bartlett (about 5 to 6 ounces each)
- 1 tablespoon fresh lemon juice
- 2 tablespoons unsalted butter, melted
- ¼ cup crumbled Roquefort or other blue cheese

In a small saucepan, combine port with ½ cup of the brown sugar. Bring to a boil over medium-high heat, stirring just to dissolve sugar. Continue to cook until mixture is slightly syrupy and reduced to ½ cup, about 5-7 minutes. Remove from heat and cool to room temperature.

Preheat oven to 425°F. Line two large baking sheets with parchment paper or foil.

Unfold thawed pastry onto a lightly floured surface. Roll out to a 10½-inch square. Cut out four 5-inch rounds and place rounds on prepared baking sheets. Pierce all over with tines of a fork. Place baking sheets in freezer while preparing fruit.

Remove stems from figs and cut each into 4 wedges; set aside. Peel, halve and core pears. Brush cut sides with lemon juice.

To assemble tarts, cut each pear half into 12 thin slices and pat dry with paper towels. Arrange slices, slightly overlapping, in groups of 3, pinwheel fashion, over each pastry round. Tuck in 4 fig wedges between the groups of pear slices to cover pastry.

Brush with melted butter and sprinkle with remaining brown sugar.

Bake 15-18 minutes until pastry is golden and pears have softened. For a more heavily glazed topping, remove baking sheets from oven and raise temperature to broil.

Slide tarts onto a clean baking sheet without the parchment paper and place under broiler for 1 minute or until pears begin to brown at the edges. Watch carefully to prevent burning.

To serve, place warm pear tarts on dessert plates, sprinkle each tart with some blue cheese and spoon port syrup around the tarts.

LOEWS GIORGIO HOTEL

Denver, Colorado

EXECUTIVE CHEF AND DIRECTOR OF FOOD AND BEVERAGE TIM FIELDS

Chef Fields' personality and cooking philosophy are clearly reflected in the menu of the hotel's **Tuscany** restaurant. Fields spent months researching the cuisine and cooking techniques of the Tuscan region of Italy and then guided his kitchen staff through the development and testing of recipes. The result is a menu that is undeniably Tuscan, but with Fields' fresh approach to ingredients and presentation. Chef Fields received top honors at the Culinary Arts Salon sponsored by the Colorado Chefs de Cuisine Association, and he was named "Chef of the Year" by the Colorado Hotel and Lodging Association.

Boasting an overall Italian theme, this 183-room property in Denver's exclusive Cherry Creek district also provides 5,000 square feet of meeting space in eight banquet rooms, a BUSINESS CENTER, and complimentary access and shuttle to BALLY'S TOTAL FITNESS CENTER. The TUSCANY restaurant offers superb Northern Italian cuisine and a selection of Italian wines that has earned it numerous awards, including five-star reviews from *The Denver Post* and *Creme de la Creme* magazine.

Small cheer and great welcome make a merry feast.
—Shakespeare

TUSCAN WARM
SUMMER SALAD

Serves 6

4 large roasted garlic cloves*

¼ pound pancetta, diced [see NOTE]

¼ cup crumbled Gorgonzola cheese

¼ cup olive oil

12 cups torn bite-size pieces romaine lettuce

4 cups torn bite-size pieces radicchio

1 cup focaccia croutons**

18 large spears Belgian endive

Place a large wok over a gas or electric burner and let it warm over medium heat 1 minute. Add garlic, pancetta, Gorgonzola and oil simultaneously. With a spoon and fork, toss mixture until the cheese is melting and the mixture starts to sizzle. Immediately add romaine and radicchio, tossing together swiftly. Once lettuces start to warm up, but just before they start to wilt, remove from heat, and add croutons; toss to combine.

To serve, place 3 endive spears each in large shallow bowls. Divide salad mixture evenly over endive spears. Serve at once.

*To make roasted garlic, remove papery outer covering of whole garlic head, but do not separate or peel the cloves. Place in a piece of heavy-duty foil, drizzle with a bit of olive oil and crumple foil around garlic to enclose. Bake in a preheated 375°F. oven 1-1¼ hours. Separate the cloves. Holding each clove, squeeze to remove the garlic puree. This is delicious spread over buttered toast or used as an ingredient in other recipes.

**To make croutons, cut focaccia or country-style bread into ¾-inch cubes. Add 1 tablespoon olive oil and some minced garlic for every cup of croutons. Spread in a single layer in a jelly-roll pan and bake in a preheated 375°F. oven 15-18 minutes until golden.

NOTE: Pancetta is Italian bacon and can be found in Italian delicatessens and specialty stores. If it is not available, lean slab bacon of excellent quality is an acceptable substitute.

PORCINI MUSHROOM RISOTTO

In a medium bowl, combine Porcini with hot water. Let stand until softened, about 30 minutes. Drain through a paper towel-lined strainer set over a small bowl. Coarsely chop mushrooms and pour soaking liquid into a measuring cup, discarding any sediment in bowl; reserve soaking liquid. There should be 1 cup.

In a medium saucepan, bring the reserved Porcini liquid and the chicken stock to a boil; adjust heat to maintain a slow, steady simmer.

In a large, heavy skillet over medium heat, melt ¼ cup (4 tablespoons) butter. Add the onion and sauté until tender. Add the rice and stir to coat with butter. Add 1 cup hot broth to just cover the rice. Adjust heat to maintain a slow simmer and cook, stirring constantly, until all the broth has been absorbed, about 3-4 minutes. Repeat process of adding hot broth about a ½ cup at a time, until the rice is tender, the mixture is creamy and the rice begins to pull away from the sides of the pan, about 25 minutes. Add remaining 2 tablespoons butter, chopped Porcini, parsley and ¼ cup Parmigiano-Reggiano. Cover and let stand off heat for 2 minutes. Spoon into shallow bowls and serve at once with additional cheese and a few grindings of black pepper

Serves 6

1½	ounces dried Porcini mushrooms
1½	cups hot water
6	tablespoons unsalted butter
½	cup finely chopped onion
1½	cups Arborio rice
4½-5	cups chicken stock or canned low-sodium chicken broth
1	cup freshly grated Parmigiano-Reggiano cheese
3	tablespoons chopped fresh parsley
	Freshly ground black pepper

ESPRESSO CHOCOLATE TORTE

Serves 16

1 cup water

2 tablespoons instant espresso coffee powder

1 cup granulated sugar

16 ounces semi-sweet chocolate, cut into chunks

2 cups (4 sticks) unsalted butter, softened and cut into pats

8 large eggs, at room temperature

¼ teaspoon salt

Raspberry Coulis (page 62)

Fresh raspberries

Confectioners sugar

Preheat oven to 350°F. Butter a 9 x 3-inch spring-form pan. Line with parchment paper; butter paper.

In a 3-quart, heavy saucepan, combine water with espresso coffee powder. Bring to a boil, stirring to dissolve the espresso; lower heat. Add sugar and chocolate and cook over low heat, stirring constantly, until sugar is dissolved and chocolate has melted. Add butter, stir until melted and mixture is smooth; remove from heat and cool slightly.

In a medium bowl, beat eggs lightly with the salt, using a wire whisk, until just combined. Stir into cooled chocolate mixture. Pour into prepared pan.

Bake 1 hour or until cake tester inserted near center comes out clean. Cool completely on wire rack. Cake will rise to top of pan and will sink slightly during cooling.

Cover and refrigerate until cold, several hours or overnight.

To serve, pool some Raspberry Coulis onto dessert plates. Cut cake into thin wedges using a knife dipped into warm water and wiped dry. Place wedge of cake on coulis, garnish with raspberries and dust lightly with confectioners sugar. Store cake in refrigerator.

A MENU FOR SPRING

MIXED GREENS WITH
HERBED VINAIGRETTE
(*page 18*)

COD FILLET WITH
EGGPLANT CAVIAR
ON ROASTED TOMATOES

ROAST PORK WITH FENNEL

GRILLED NEW POTATO AND
ASPARAGUS SALAD

GRANPA'S WITH
CHANTILLY CREAM

COD FILLET
WITH EGGPLANT CAVIAR ON
ROASTED TOMATOES

Serves 6

18 roasted tomato halves [see NOTE]

2 purple eggplants (1 pound each)

2 tablespoons olive oil

Salt and freshly ground black pepper

1 teaspoon minced fresh garlic

6 cod fillets, ³/₄-inch thick and about 7 inches long (6 ounces each), bones removed

2 tablespoons unsalted butter, plus some for coating baking dish

Chervil sprigs for garnish

Prepare roasted tomatoes.

Preheat oven to 400°F.

Cut eggplants in half lengthwise. Place, cut-side up, on a large, shallow baking pan and brush with olive oil. Sprinkle with salt and pepper. Let stand a few minutes. Bake eggplant 30-35 minutes or until soft and brown on undersides. Remove from oven and let cool 10 minutes. Reduce oven temperature to 375°F.

When eggplant is cool enough to handle, remove meat from skin and place in a medium bowl. Add garlic and mash as smooth as possible; add salt and pepper to taste.

Using a small sharp knife, butterfly cod fillets by slitting them in half lengthwise leaving one side attached. Open fillets up and spread bottom half of each fillet with ¼ cup of the eggplant puree; fold other half over the filling.

Lightly butter a shallow baking dish large enough to hold fillets in a single layer. Place stuffed fillets in dish, sprinkle with salt and pepper and dot with butter. Bake 15 minutes or until fish flakes easily with a fork and filling is hot. If desired, place under broiler for a few minutes to lightly brown top of fillets.

To serve, place 4 roasted tomato halves in a diagonal row on each dinner plate. Place fillet slightly off center of tomatoes and garnish with chervil sprigs.

NOTE: To make roasted tomato halves, place large halved plum tomatoes, cut-side up, on a lightly oiled jelly-roll pan. Brush with olive oil and sprinkle with salt and pepper. Roast in a preheated 475°F. oven 1 hour and 10 minutes until tomato halves are dark brown. Herbs, such as rosemary, thyme, chives or cilantro, can also be sprinkled over tomato halves before roasting.

ROAST PORK WITH FENNEL

Preheat oven to 375°F.

In a small cup, combine garlic, rosemary, fennel seeds, 1 teaspoon salt and ⅛ teaspoon pepper. Rub herb mixture on surface of meat. Place 1 tablespoon butter and the olive oil in a shallow roasting pan. Place pork, fat-side up, in pan without rack. Insert a meat thermometer in center of roast, making sure bulb does not touch fat or bone. Roast, uncovered, 1½ hours or until meat thermometer registers 150°F.

Meanwhile, cut off the feathery fronds and stalks from the fennel bulb and remove any tough outer layers. Roughly chop the fennel bulb. Place in a medium saucepan with remaining 2 tablespoons butter and 1 cup of water. Bring to a boil, reduce heat and cook, covered, until tender, about 25-30 minutes. Process in food processor with milk until slightly chunky. Return to saucepan.

Remove roast to platter when done and cover loosely with foil; allow to rest 15 minutes.

Pour off fat from roasting pan, leaving meat juices in pan. Return 1 tablespoon fat to pan. Stir in flour to make a smooth mixture. Gradually whisk in wine and bring to a boil, stirring – mixture will thicken slightly. Strain into saucepan with the fennel. Heat over low heat to serving temperature. Taste for salt and pepper.

To serve, slice pork and arrange on a large serving platter. Spoon over some of the sauce. Pass remainder in a sauce boat.

Serves 6

1 tablespoon finely chopped garlic

1 teaspoon finely chopped fresh rosemary

1 teaspoon fennel seeds, slightly crushed

Salt and freshly ground black pepper

1 3-3½ pound (6-rib) loin of pork, bones split by butcher

2 tablespoons unsalted butter

1 tablespoon extra-virgin olive oil

1 fennel bulb (about 1 pound)

½ cup milk

1 tablespoon all-purpose flour

1 cup dry white wine

GRILLED NEW POTATO AND ASPARAGUS SALAD

Serves 4 to 6

2 pounds medium-size new potatoes, scrubbed and quartered

3 tablespoons olive oil

2 teaspoons minced garlic

Salt and freshly ground black pepper

1 pound medium-size asparagus spears, washed and trimmed

¼ cup chopped red onion

¼ cup chopped scallions

¼ cup chopped oil-packed sun-dried tomatoes, drained

2 teaspoons finely chopped fresh basil

Prepare a medium-hot fire in a covered charcoal or gas grill.

In a large bowl, combine potatoes, 2 tablespoons oil, garlic, ½ teaspoon salt and ¼ teaspoon pepper; toss to coat. Place potatoes on an oiled grill and cook, covered, until lightly browned and tender when pierced with a fork, 15-20 minutes. Turn several times with a spatula for even cooking. Transfer to a bowl; cover loosely with foil to keep warm.

Brush asparagus with remaining 1 tablespoon oil and sprinkle with salt and pepper. Lay the asparagus perpendicular to the long grids so they don't fall through the grill, turning often with tongs until softened and tinged with brown. Cut into 3 to 4 diagonal pieces. Add to potatoes with red onion, scallions, sun-dried tomatoes, and basil; toss lightly to combine. Add salt and pepper to taste.

GRANPA'S

These puffy, nutmeg–scented dumplings are a traditional specialty
of Canada and the North Country of the United States

Make Chantilly Cream and refrigerate.

In a large, wide saucepan, combine maple syrup with water; cover and bring to a boil over medium heat, about 10 minutes.

Meanwhile, in a large bowl, combine flour, sugar, baking powder, salt and nutmeg. Cut in 2 tablespoons butter with a pastry blender or two knives used scissor-fashion. Stir in milk, mixing with a fork just until blended. Drop batter by 6 large rounded tablespoonfuls onto gently boiling maple syrup mixture. Cover tightly and simmer 15 minutes. DO NOT PEEK. Gently lift dumplings out, one at a time, placing one in each of 6 shallow bowls.

Remove any loose bits of cooked dough from syrup with a slotted spoon. Stir remaining 2 tablespoons butter into hot syrup until melted. Top each dumpling with ¼ cup syrup, some Chantilly Cream and mixed fresh berries. Serve at once.

Serves 6

Chantilly Cream (recipe follows)

2 cups maple syrup

2 cups water

2 cups all-purpose flour

2 tablespoons sugar

4 teaspoons baking powder

1 teaspoon salt

½ teaspoon freshly grated nutmeg

¼ cup (½ stick) unsalted butter

1 cup milk

Mixed fresh berries

CHANTILLY CREAM

Place all ingredients in small bowl of electric mixer. Beat at high speed just until stiff peaks form. Refrigerate until ready to use.

Makes 4 cups

1 pint (2 cups) heavy cream

¼ cup sugar

1 teaspoon vanilla

Loews L'Enfant Plaza Hotel

Washington, D.C.

EXECUTIVE CHEF EVAN PERCOCO

Before joining **Loews L'Enfant Plaza Hotel,** Chef Percoco had been the Resident Chef for Saudi Arabian Prince Khalid Al-Faisal at his official residence outside Washington. Prior to that, this graduate of the Culinary Institute of America was the Executive Sous Chef at the Mayflower Hotel and had also worked at many New York City restaurants before moving to the nation's capital. Reflecting on his father's preparation of traditional Italian holiday dinners, Chef Percoco credits him for his own appreciation of cuisine. Chef Percoco's favorite ingredient? Butter! He also likes to use the fresh herbs and vegetables he grows in his own garden.

In the nation's capital, Loews L'Enfant Plaza Hotel is convenient to the national monuments, air and space exhibits, the Smithsonian, the National Gallery, and Capitol Hill. Its 370 rooms and suites are complemented by more than 21,000 square feet of meeting space, a full-service Executive Business Center, fitness center and an all-season rooftop pool. The contemporary American grill Cafe Pierre offers such distinctive dining areas as The Terrace, an elegant setting for à la carte and prix fixe menus, a more informal American Brasserie and the Lobby Cafe, serving breakfast, salads, sandwiches, and light fare throughout the day.

> *Butter! Give me butter! Always butter!*
> —Fernand Point

FETTUCCINE WITH VEGETABLES AND
WHITE WINE BASIL BUTTER

This dish becomes a main course with the addition of cooked fresh shrimp.
Add them to the sauce along with the vegetables just before serving.

Serves 6

1   pound slender asparagus, trimmed and cut into 1-inch bias pieces

1   cup broccoli florets

1   (12 ounces) package fettuccine

3   tablespoons olive oil

1   cup assorted wild mushrooms, such as Shiitake and Cremini, cleaned, trimmed, and cut into thin slices

½   cup red onion slivers

4   cloves garlic, peeled and thinly sliced

1   cup dry white wine

½   cup (1 stick) unsalted butter, cut into small pieces

10   sun-dried tomatoes in oil, drained and julienned

½   cup chiffonade of fresh basil

Salt and freshly ground black pepper

In a large saucepot, bring 5 quarts of salted water to a boil. Fill a large bowl with ice and water. Add asparagus and broccoli to boiling water; cook 1 minute or so until vegetables are bright green. Remove with a wide-mesh strainer and place into ice water to stop cooking; drain and set aside.

When water returns to boiling in saucepot, add pasta and cook to *al dente* stage, about 13 minutes.

While pasta is cooking, heat oil in a large skillet over medium heat. Add mushrooms and sauté until browned, about 3-4 minutes. Add onion and garlic, and sauté 2-3 minutes. Add wine and reduce by ½ over high heat, about 5 minutes. Reduce heat to low and add butter. Cook and stir until melted. Add asparagus, broccoli and tomatoes (and shrimp, if using). Heat 1 minute.

Drain pasta. Place in large bowl. Add vegetable mixture; toss to combine. Add basil and salt and pepper to taste. Toss again.

PAN-ROASTED DUCK BREAST
WITH HERBED WILD RICE PANCAKE AND
DRIED FRUIT PECAN COMPOTE

Prepare Dried Fruit Pecan Compote according to recipe.

In a medium bowl, combine flour, baking powder, sugar, salt and pepper with a whisk. Add cooked wild rice, chives, chopped thyme and rosemary; mix to combine. In a small bowl, beat egg with milk and melted butter. Add to flour mixture all at once, whisking just until smooth.

Heat a nonstick griddle over low heat. To test temperature, drop a little cold water onto griddle; water should roll off in drops. For each pancake, pour 1/4 cup batter onto griddle. Cook until bubbles form on surface, edges become dry and underside is nicely browned, about 1 1/2-2 minutes. Turn, and cook until brown, about 1 minute. Transfer to a plate; keep warm. Makes 6 pancakes.*

Remove excess fat from duck. Rinse under cold water and pat dry with paper towels. Sprinkle with additional salt and pepper. Heat a heavy (preferably cast iron) skillet over high heat. Brush lightly with oil. Place duck breasts, skin-side down, in hot skillet. Cook until skin is brown and crisp, about 6 minutes. Turn and cook to desired doneness, about 3-4 minutes or longer for medium-rare. Remove duck breasts to a plate; let rest 5 minutes. Thinly slice duck breasts, keeping each one separate.

To serve, place a warm pancake in center of plate. Place 1 1/2 tablespoons Dried Fruit Pecan Compote in center of pancake. Arrange slices of one duck breast around pancake. Garnish with fresh herb sprigs.

*Pancakes may be made ahead and refrigerated. Cover with foil and heat in a 350°F. oven 8-10 minutes until hot.

Serves 6

Dried Fruit Pecan Compote (recipe follows)

3/4	cup all-purpose flour
1/2	teaspoon baking powder
1/2	teaspoon sugar
1/4	teaspoon salt
1/4	teaspoon freshly ground black pepper
1/2	cup cooked wild rice
1/4	cup snipped chives
1	teaspoon minced fresh thyme plus 6 small sprigs for garnish
1	teaspoon minced fresh rosemary plus 6 small sprigs for garnish
1	large egg
2/3	cup milk
2	tablespoons unsalted butter, melted and cooled
6	boneless duck breast halves, skin on (about 6 ounces each)
	Vegetable oil

DRIED FRUIT PECAN COMPOTE

In a medium-size saucepan, combine wine with sugar. Bring to a boil over high heat, stirring until sugar is dissolved. Cook over high heat 6-7 minutes until reduced to 1 1/2 cups. Add remaining ingredients; cook and stir 1 minute longer. Remove from heat. Transfer to a bowl. Let cool. Compote will thicken upon standing. Cover and refrigerate until ready to use. Serve at room temperature.

Makes 2 1/2 cups

1 1/2	cups dry red wine
1 1/4	cups sugar
3/4	cup pecan pieces, coarsely chopped
2/3	cup sun-dried cranberries
1/2	cup sun-dried blueberries
1/2	cup golden raisins

STRAWBERRY SHORTCAKE

Serves 6 to 8

Chantilly Cream (page 53)

1¹/₂ cups all-purpose flour

¹/₃ cup plus ¹/₂ cup sugar

1¹/₂ teaspoons baking powder

¹/₂ teaspoon baking soda

9 tablespoons (1 stick plus 1 tablespoon) unsalted butter, softened

¹/₂ cup milk

¹/₄ cup fresh orange juice

¹/₄ cup white rum

1 tablespoon vanilla

1 quart strawberries, washed, hulled and quartered

Confectioners sugar

Mint sprigs for garnish

Prepare Chantilly Cream and refrigerate.

Preheat oven to 400°F. Line a large baking sheet with parchment paper.

In a large bowl, sift together flour, ¹/₃ cup sugar, baking powder and baking soda. With a pastry blender or two knives used scissor-fashion, cut in 7 tablespoons of butter until mixture resembles coarse cornmeal. Add milk all at once, stirring with a fork just until dough cleans sides of bowl. Drop in 6 to 8 mounds onto prepared baking sheet, about 2 inches apart. Bake 12-15 minutes or until light golden. Transfer to a wire rack.

Meanwhile, in a large skillet, place remaining 2 tablespoons butter, remaining ¹/₂ cup sugar, orange juice, rum and vanilla. Bring to a boil over high heat. Stand back as the mixture may flame. If it does, the flame will burn itself out in a few seconds. Cook and stir over high heat until mixture gets slightly syrupy, about 3-5 minutes. Remove from heat; add strawberries and gently toss to coat.

To assemble, split warm shortcakes in half crosswise. Place some Chantilly Cream on each dessert plate. Place bottom halves of shortcakes, cut side up, on top of cream. Cover with some of the warm strawberry mixture. Top with more of the cream. Set top of shortcake over cream. Dust lightly with confectioners sugar. Garnish with mint sprig.

LOEWS SANTA MONICA BEACH HOTEL

Los Angeles, California

CHEF DIRECTOR ALAIN GIRAUD

With the culinary flair inherent in his French roots and training, Chef Giraud has brought a new generation of cuisine to this oceanfront luxury hotel with the new restaurant **Lavande**. Born in Paris, Giraud credits both of his grandmothers for his inspiration to pursue a career in the culinary arts. He perfected his skills in some of the most venerable Michelin-starred restaurants in France, including L'Hermitage Messonnier in Avignon and the Hotel Crillon and Le Grand Vefour in Paris. After moving to Los Angeles, Chef Giraud joined Michel Richard at the highly regarded Citrus restaurant, where he was Executive Chef. An avid fisherman, Giraud also collects old and rare cookery books.

They dined on mince, and slices of quince
which they ate with a runcible spoon;
And, hand in hand, on the edge of the sand,
they danced by the light of the moon.
—Lewis Carroll

The sun, the beach, the historic Pier, and shopping make Santa Monica a perfect spot from which to explore the environs of Los Angeles; Beverly Hills and West L.A. are minutes away. And, with its prime beachfront location, Loews Santa Monica Beach Hotel offers the ideal base for exploring or for simply settling into sybaritic luxury. There are 343 rooms and 24 suites at ocean side, an indoor/outdoor pool, a full-service health and fitness spa and 17,000 square feet of space to accommodate groups of up to 900 guests. Overlooking the magnificent Pacific, the hotel's restaurant Lavande blends Provençal-style cuisine with California flavors in light, sun-kissed dishes.

SQUID AND POTATOES
WITH ROUILLE

Serves 8

6   garlic cloves, peeled

Salt

2   large egg yolks, at room temperature

2   tablespoons water, plus 2 cups

2   tablespoons fresh lemon juice

¼   teaspoon sugar

1   teaspoon dry mustard

½   teaspoon cayenne

1   cup olive oil, <u>not</u> extra-virgin, plus ¼ cup

2   cups diced onion

2   tablespoons tomato paste

4   large, vine-ripened tomatoes (about 7 ounces each), cored and coarsely chopped

2   cups dry white wine

1   tablespoon finely chopped fresh thyme

1   bay leaf

2   pounds yellow potatoes, pared and cut into ½-inch dice

2   pounds cleaned squid, cut into ½-inch slices

Freshly ground black pepper

Chopped parsley for garnish

In a mortar, pound 3 garlic cloves with ¼ teaspoon salt to a paste or, on a work surface, finely chop together and work into a smooth paste by using the side of a knife; set aside.

Finely chop remaining garlic and set aside.

Fill a shallow bowl with ice and water and set aside. In a small skillet, combine egg yolks, 2 tablespoons water, lemon juice and sugar. Place over low heat and stir constantly to warm the yolks. Remove skillet from heat at the first sign of thickening and set over the ice and water to stop cooking, stirring constantly. Pour into blender container, cover and blend a few seconds until eggs are foamy, light yellow in color and cool. Add mustard and cayenne; cover. With motor running, add ½ cup of the olive oil, drop by drop, through feeder hole in center of blender cover. After ½ cup of the oil has been incorporated, the sauce will thicken. At this point, add another ½ cup in a slow, steady stream until mixture looks like a thick heavy cream.* Transfer to a bowl and stir in garlic paste; cover with plastic wrap and refrigerate.

In a large saucepot, heat remaining ¼ cup oil; sauté remaining chopped garlic with the onions until tender, about 10 minutes. Stir in tomato paste. Add tomatoes, wine, remaining 2 cups water, thyme and bay leaf and bring to a boil over medium-high heat; reduce heat. Add potatoes and squid and simmer, covered, 45 minutes until squid and potatoes are tender. Add salt and pepper to taste. Remove bay leaf.

To serve, ladle soup into shallow soup bowls. Sprinkle with parsley. Pass the bowl of rouille and let guests help themselves to swirl as much as they wish into their soup bowls.

*If the rouille has not thickened at this point, warm a small mixing bowl with warm water and dry. Add 1 teaspoon of Dijon mustard and 1 teaspoon of the thin rouille and beat with a wire whisk until mustard and rouille cream together; beat in the rest of the sauce by tablespoons, thickening each addition before adding the next.

ROASTED SALMON
WITH ARTICHOKES BARIGOULE

Prepare a large bowl of cold water mixed with the lemon juice. Cut the baby artichokes in half lengthwise, trim off any sharp points on leaves and scoop out fibrous chokes, if any, with a spoon. Drop trimmed artichokes into lemon-water to prevent discoloration.

In a large skillet, heat 1 teaspoon of olive oil over medium heat. Add bacon and cook until slightly browned, about 3 minutes. Add carrots, onions and garlic; sauté until tender, about 3 minutes. Drain artichokes and pat dry on paper towels. Add them to the skillet along with the thyme sprigs and basil branches; toss to combine. Add wine and bring to a boil over high heat; reduce liquid to half, about 5 minutes. Add chicken stock and cook until artichokes are tender, about 8-10 minutes. Remove and discard thyme and basil branches.

Meanwhile, preheat oven to 350°F.

Sprinkle salmon with salt and pepper. In a large skillet, heat 1 teaspoon oil over high heat; add fillets and brown on both sides, about 2 minutes. Transfer to a shallow baking dish just large enough to hold salmon in a single layer. Place in oven and bake 5 minutes or until fish flakes easily with a fork.

While fish is baking, plunge basil leaves into boiling water in a small saucepan; drain, then plunge into ice and water, drain again. Finely chop basil leaves and stir into hot artichoke barigoule with the remaining oil just before serving. Taste for salt and pepper.

To serve, spoon barigoule into 4 oversized bowls; top each with a roasted salmon fillet.

Serves 4

1	teaspoon lemon juice
12	baby artichokes, walnut-size
1/4	cup olive oil
1	slice bacon, diced
1/2	cup thinly sliced carrots
1/2	cup thinly sliced onion
4	garlic cloves, thinly sliced
2	sprigs fresh thyme
1	cup small fresh basil leaves, branches reserved
1	cup dry white wine
1 1/2	cups chicken stock or canned low-sodium chicken broth
4	salmon fillets (6 ounces each)
	Salt and freshly ground black pepper

INDIVIDUAL HOT FUDGE CHOCOLATE CAKES

*These rich, lavender-scented chocolate fudge cakes
have a pudding-like center.*

Serves 6

Raspberry Coulis (recipe follows)

Unsweetened cocoa powder for dusting ramekins

6 ounces bittersweet chocolate, coarsely chopped

1½ teaspoons dried lavender, tied in a piece of cheesecloth

1 cup (2 sticks) unsalted butter, cut up

3 large eggs, at room temperature

3 large egg yolks, at room temperature

¼ cup granulated sugar

⅓ cup all-purpose flour

Confectioners sugar

Prepare Raspberry Coulis and refrigerate.

Preheat oven to 400°F. Lightly coat the insides of six straight-sided ramekins (3½ x 1½-inches) with butter. Dust with cocoa; tap out excess. Set on a jelly-roll pan.

In top of double boiler over simmering water, place chocolate with lavender sachet and melt chocolate, stirring occasionally, until smooth. Add butter and stir until melted and mixture is smooth. Remove from heat; cool. Remove lavender sachet and discard.

In bowl with electric mixer on high speed, beat eggs, egg yolks and granulated sugar until triple in volume, light lemony in color and mixture is thick enough to form a slowly dissolving ribbon when the beaters are lifted, about 3-4 minutes. On low speed, add cooled chocolate mixture. Add flour and beat until most of the flour is incorporated. Using a rubber spatula, fold the chocolate and flour completely into the beaten eggs. Divide batter evenly among prepared ramekins.

Bake 14 minutes until cakes puff like soufflés and are set on top. Remove from oven and let stand 2-3 minutes. The cakes will deflate slightly. Run a small knife around the side of ramekins to loosen each cake. Using a mitt, gently turn ramekin over onto parchment or waxed paper and lift edge with knife to remove from ramekin.

While cakes are cooling, pool Raspberry Coulis on dessert plates. Transfer each warm cake onto coulis using a large spatula. Dust lightly with confectioners sugar. Serve at once.

RASPBERRY COULIS

Makes 1½ cups

2 cups fresh raspberries

½ cup granulated sugar

¼ teaspoon fresh lemon juice

In blender or food processor, puree raspberries with sugar until smooth. Strain through a fine sieve set over a bowl. Stir in lemon juice. Cover and refrigerate until ready to use.

A Menu for Summer

Grilled Fish Tacos

Mango and Papaya Salsa

Guacamole

Salsa Borracho

Portobello
Goat Cheese Burger on
Herbed Focaccia

Ice Cream Sundaes

Thumbprint Cookies

GRILLED FISH TACOS

Serves 4

2 1½ to 2-pound whole bass or snapper, cleaned and scales removed

Salt and freshly ground black pepper

Fresh thyme

Fresh dill

2 bay leaves

8 garlic cloves, peeled

2 tablespoons olive oil

Mango and Papaya Salsa (recipe follows)

8-10 corn or flour tortillas (8-inch)

2 cups shredded iceberg lettuce

1 cup coarsely chopped plum tomatoes

½ cup coarsely chopped fresh cilantro

Guacamole (recipe follows)

Salsa Borracho (recipe follows)

Prepare a medium-hot fire in a charcoal or gas grill or preheat broiler.

Rinse each fish, inside and out, with cold water; pat dry with paper towels.

Sprinkle cavity and fish with salt and pepper. Stuff each fish cavity with a handful of thyme and dill, a bay leaf and 4 garlic cloves; rub with oil. Place fish in a fish basket and place on grill. Grill each side 8-10 minutes or until fish flakes easily with a fork. If using a broiler, cook the fish in a shallow nonstick baking pan, 4 to 6 inches from heat source, turning once. Remove from heat and place on a warm platter. When the fish is cool enough to handle, remove skin and bones; flake into large pieces. Keep warm.

Meanwhile, heat tortillas following package directions. Place 2 tablespoons of Mango and Papaya Salsa on each tortilla. Top with lettuce, tomatoes, flaked fish and cilantro. Top with more salsa, Guacamole or Salsa Borracho. Fold over to form a taco.

MANGO AND PAPAYA SALSA

In a medium bowl, combine all ingredients; mix lightly to blend. Cover and refrigerate until ready to use.

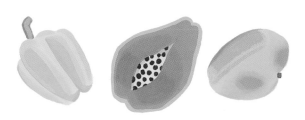

Makes 3½ cups

1 medium-size, ripe mango (about 1 pound), peeled, pitted and diced

1 medium-size, ripe papaya, strawberry variety if possible (about 1 pound), peeled, seeded and diced

½ cup seeded and diced red bell pepper

½ cup seeded and diced yellow bell pepper

1 tablespoon seeded and minced jalapeño pepper

1 tablespoon finely chopped fresh cilantro

2 tablespoons fresh lime juice

GUACAMOLE

In a 3- quart saucepan, bring water to a boil. Stir in salt and add tomatillos. Bring back to a boil; reduce heat and simmer 10 minutes until tomatillos are soft; drain. Place tomatillos in blender or food processor and puree until smooth; cool.

In a medium-size mixing bowl, coarsely mash the avocados with a fork. Stir in pureed tomatillos with cilantro, onion and jalapeño pepper. Taste for salt and pepper.

Cover with plastic wrap and refrigerate until ready to use.

Makes 3½ cups

1 quart water

1 tablespoon salt

8 tomatillos (about ½ pound), husked

4 ripe avocados, preferably Hass (8 ounces each)

½ cup coarsely chopped fresh cilantro

½ cup minced onion

1½ tablespoons seeded and minced jalapeño pepper

Salt and freshly ground black pepper

SALSA BORRACHO

This salsa is more like a condiment to add heat to your taco.
You can leave the seeds of the jalapeño pepper in or, for a milder taste, remove them.

Makes 2⅔ cups

- 3   medium, ripe tomatoes (6 ounces each)
- 2   large, dried New Mexico chiles
- 1   large, dried ancho chile
- 1   cup boiling water
- ⅓   cup finely chopped onion
- ⅓   cup finely chopped fresh cilantro
- 1   tablespoon finely chopped fresh garlic
- 1   coarsely chopped jalapeño pepper, seeded if desired
- ¼   cup gold tequila
- 3   tablespoons fresh lime juice
- ¾   teaspoon salt

Preheat broiler. Place tomatoes on a shallow broiler pan and broil for 20 minutes or until tomato skins have blackened. Remove from broiler and let cool to room temperature.

Meanwhile, heat a heavy skillet or griddle over medium heat. Toast the New Mexico and ancho chiles a few minutes on each side to soften and warm them. Do not let blacken or they will impart a bitter taste to the salsa. Stem, seed and tear chiles into small pieces. Place in a heatproof bowl. Pour over boiling water; cool to room temperature. Drain, reserving 3 tablespoons of the soaking liquid.

Core tomatoes and coarsely chop. Place in a large food processor with their blackened skins and juices, the chile pieces and the reserved 3 tablespoons soaking liquid, onion, cilantro, garlic, jalapeño peppers, tequila, lime juice and salt. Pulse until the mixture is fairly smooth. Place in a bowl; cover and refrigerate at least 30 minutes or until ready to serve.

PORTOBELLO GOAT CHEESE BURGER
on HERBED FOCACCIA

Preheat grill or broiler.

In a small bowl, combine goat cheese, cream cheese, 1 teaspoon minced garlic, basil and 1 teaspoon olive oil, mixing well. Let stand at room temperature for flavors to mellow.

In a small cup, combine the remaining 3 tablespoons of oil, 4 teaspoons minced garlic and the thyme. Brush mixture over the mushrooms. Let marinate at room temperature 10 minutes. Grill or broil until soft, about 10-12 minutes, turning once. Season with salt and pepper to taste; keep warm.

Place the warmed focaccia on serving plates. Top with a mushroom, some of the goat cheese mixture and mesclun.

Serves 4

2 ounces California goat cheese, softened to room temperature

2 ounces cream cheese, softened to room temperature

5 teaspoons minced garlic

1 tablespoon minced fresh basil

3 tablespoons plus 1 teaspoon olive oil

1 tablespoon minced fresh thyme

4 medium Portobello mushrooms (4 to 5 ounces each), wiped clean and stems removed

   Salt and freshly ground black pepper

4 4 x 4-inch pieces herbed focaccia, warmed

1 ounce mesclun (1 cup), washed and dried

ICE CREAM SUNDAES

Food from the grill, eaten in the open air, is an American summer tradition. And what better way to end a 4th of July celebration or an everyday feast— indoors or out—than with another all-American favorite: Ice Cream Sundaes. The chefs of the Loews Hotels family know that Sundaes are good— whatever the season—and they always have them on the menu: Comfort food for the kid in all of us. The Loews Hotels difference? Great ice cream, real homemade toppings, delicious indulgence.

Set up a Sundae Buffet with a variety of mix and match sauces and ice creams. It's a great opportunity for culinary creativity. Here are a few ideas for a start.

· This hot-fudge-like Chocolate Sauce is good on nearly everything—try it on Banana Rum Ice Cream—and don't forget the chopped nuts and whipped cream. Serve with Thumbprint Cookies (recipe follows).

CHOCOLATE SAUCE

Makes 2½ cups

1 cup water

⅔ cup sugar

¼ cup light corn syrup

¾ cup European-style unsweetened cocoa powder, sifted after measuring

8 ounces (8 squares) semi-sweet chocolate, cut up

2 teaspoons vanilla

In a medium-size, heavy saucepan, combine water, sugar and corn syrup. Bring to a boil over medium heat, stirring just to combine ingredients. Whisk in cocoa powder until smooth; add chocolate and stir until melted. Remove from heat and stir in vanilla.

Mixture will thicken more upon cooling. Serve warm or refrigerate until ready to use. Reheat in top of a double boiler or microwave.

· The Chocolate Sauce also can be spooned over Bourbon Ice Cream (page 32) or Schnapps Ice Cream (page 15) or over softened good-quality commercial chocolate, vanilla, strawberry or peppermint ice cream combined with crushed Thin Mint wafer cookies.

BANANA RUM ICE CREAM

Allow ice cream to soften slightly at room temperature. In a small bowl, mash together the banana and the rum. You should have ⅓ to ½ cup puree. Stir mixture into the softened ice cream. Turn into a plastic freezer container and freeze until firm.

NOTE: Try this technique with other pureed fruit and different liquors or liqueurs.

Serves 4

1 pint good-quality vanilla ice cream

1 small, overripe banana [see NOTE]

2 tablespoons light rum

FRUITFUL TOPPINGS

· Fold a melange of fresh berries—blueberries, raspberries, strawberries—into Raspberry Coulis (page 62) to top ice cream or, for a lighter treat, Tequila Lime Sorbet (page 25)

· Serve the marinated Strawberries (page 58) on vanilla, strawberry or Banana Rum Ice Cream.

· Spike a mixture of tropical fruits—kiwi, mango, pineapple, bananas, etc.—with some rum or orange liqueur and serve over Mango and White Rum Sorbet (page 83) or Banana Rum Ice Cream.

THUMBPRINT COOKIES

Makes 3 dozen

1 cup (2 sticks) unsalted butter, softened

½ cup firmly packed light brown sugar

½ teaspoon salt

2 large eggs, separated

1 teaspoon almond extract

2¼ cups bread flour

1¾ cups finely chopped pecans or walnuts

Orange marmalade, raspberry, strawberry or apricot preserves

Preheat oven to 350°F.

In a large bowl, with electric mixer at medium-high speed, beat together the butter, brown sugar and salt until fluffy and light; beat in egg yolks and almond extract.

Stir in the flour, half at a time, to make a stiff dough.

Whisk egg whites in a pie plate until foamy; sprinkle nuts on waxed paper. Roll dough, using 1 level measuring tablespoon at a time, between palms of hands to make a ball; roll each in egg white, then into pecans to coat all over. Place, 2 inches apart, on large ungreased cookie sheets. Press center of each cookie with fingertip to make a little hollow. Fill hollow with a heaping ½ teaspoon of marmalade or preserve.

Bake 12-14 minutes or until firm and lightly golden. Cool completely on wire racks.

· Other cookies to accompany Ice Cream Sundaes: Chocolate Espresso Cookies (page 32) and Mexican Wedding Cakes (page 25).

Loews New York Hotel

New York, New York

**EXECUTIVE CHEF
JOHN IACHETTI**

Chef Iachetti joined **Loews New York Hotel** as Banquet Chef/ Kitchen Manager and was promoted to Executive Chef a few years later. He oversees the kitchen activities in the hotel's **Lexington Avenue Grill,** a showcase for seasonal and regional American cuisine. After Iachetti graduated from the Culinary Institute of America, he spent two years at the former Loews Glenpointe Hotel in New Jersey. His refrigerator at home holds Chef Iachetti's collection of 100 types of mustard as well as examples of his own homemade beer, pickled vegetables and preserved seasonal specialties.

At the hub of midtown Manhattan's business, cultural, and shopping districts is the 722-room Loews New York Hotel. Along with a full-service health club and the special concierge floor, Club 51, the hotel also features deluxe suites complete with Jacuzzi and sauna and a Business Center with meeting spaces for groups of 10 to 450. At the center of activity, open to the hotel's Art Deco lobby, is the Lexington Avenue Grill offering regional flavors from around the country in a menu which changes daily to reflect seasonal bounty.

In cooking, as in all the arts, simplicity is the sign of perfection.
—*Curnonsky*

LOBSTER ROLLS
WITH CORN AND TOMATO RELISH

Serves 6

4   cups cooked lobster meat (1½ pounds), cut into ½-inch pieces

1   cup finely chopped celery

1   cup finely chopped red onion

½   cup finely chopped leeks, white part only

⅓   cup mayonnaise

¼   cup fresh lemon juice

    Salt and freshly ground black pepper

2   vine-ripened tomatoes (6 ounces each)

1   ear tender fresh corn

2   tablespoons finely chopped fresh tarragon

1   tablespoon finely chopped fresh chervil

4   ounces mesclun

2   tablespoons olive oil

1   tablespoon champagne vinegar

6   large crusty club rolls (6 x 3½-inches) or roll of choice

    Potato chips

In a large bowl, combine lobster, celery, onion, leeks, mayonnaise and lemon juice; mix lightly to combine. Add salt and pepper to taste. Cover and refrigerate until ready to use.

Core, seed and coarsely chop tomatoes. Place in a medium bowl. Shuck corn, stand ear upright and, with a small knife, cut down along the cob to remove kernels. Add to tomatoes with tarragon and chervil; mix lightly to combine. Cover and refrigerate.

Just before assembling sandwich, in a medium bowl, combine mesclun with oil and vinegar. Finely chop enough mesclun to make ½ cup. Add to the tomato-corn relish.

With a serrated knife, slice off top of each roll, ⅓ of the way down. Make a hollow in the soft center in bottom of each roll (save soft crumbs for another use). Tuck some of the mesclun in bottom of roll; mound lobster salad over greens. Cover with top of roll. Serve with tomato-corn relish and potato chips.

ROAST PRIME RIB AU JUS WITH HORSERADISH MASHED POTATOES

Position oven rack in lower third of the oven. Preheat oven to 325°F.

Wipe roast with dampened paper towels. Rub roast with salt and pepper. Set roast on its ribs, fat-side up, in a shallow roasting pan. Insert a meat thermometer in center of roast, making sure bulb does not touch fat or bone. For medium-rare, roast 2¼-2½ hours or until meat thermometer registers 135°F. For medium, roast 2¾-3 hours or until meat thermometer registers 150°F. Remove roast to a serving platter and cover lightly with foil to rest for 15-20 minutes.

Pour off fat from roasting pan. Place pan over medium heat. Whisk in beef stock or broth, scraping up browned bits in pan. Bring to a boil. Taste, adding salt and pepper, if needed. Strain gravy into a sauce boat and serve with rib roast and Horseradish Mashed Potatoes.

Serves 8 generously

1   3-rib beef roast (7 to 8 pounds), cut from small end, with chine bone removed by butcher

   Salt and freshly ground black pepper

2   cups beef stock or canned low-sodium beef broth

   Horseradish Mashed Potatoes (recipe follows)

HORSERADISH MASHED POTATOES

Preheat oven to 325°F.

Peel potatoes and cut into large chunks. Cook, covered, in 1 inch boiling water until tender, about 15-20 minutes; drain. Put potatoes on a jelly-roll pan in oven 5-6 minutes to dry.

In a small saucepan, warm cream with butter and horserad-ish until butter is melted.

In a large bowl, mash potatoes with electric mixer or potato masher. Gradually add warm cream mixture, beating constantly, until potatoes are fluffy and creamy. Stir in rosemary. Season with salt and pepper.

Serves 8

7-8   large yellow potatoes, such as Yukon Gold, (3 pounds)

1   cup heavy cream

6   tablespoons salted butter

3-4   tablespoons prepared white horseradish, drained

2-3   tablespoons finely chopped fresh rosemary

   Salt and freshly ground black pepper

APPLE BROWN BETTY with CINNAMON ICE CREAM

The chef uses Irish soda bread crumbs to top this delicious dish.
Buy Irish soda bread without caraway seeds at the bake shop, or make your favorite recipe.
The addition of raisins in the bread adds to the flavor.

Serves 8

- 2 cups fresh bread crumbs, preferably Irish soda bread without caraway seeds
- 3 large McIntosh apples (1¼ pounds), peeled, cored and thinly sliced
- 3 large Winesap apples (1¼ pounds), peeled, cored and thinly sliced
- ⅓ cup firmly packed dark brown sugar
- ⅓ cup granulated sugar
- 1 tablespoon fresh lemon juice
- 1 teaspoon vanilla
- ¼ teaspoon freshly grated nutmeg
- ½ cup (1 stick) unsalted butter, melted
- 1 pint cinnamon or other ice cream [see NOTE]

Preheat oven to 450°F.

Spread fresh bread crumbs on jelly-roll pan and toast for 5 minutes, just until crumbs begin to dry but are not brown. Remove from oven and cool. Reduce oven temperature to 375°F. Butter an 8-inch square baking dish.

In a large bowl, place apples, brown sugar, granulated sugar, lemon juice, vanilla and nutmeg; toss gently to combine. In a small bowl, combine bread crumbs with melted butter, mixing lightly just to moisten.

Sprinkle ½ cup of the bread crumbs in bottom of prepared dish. Top with apple mixture; sprinkle with remaining crumbs. Cover dish tightly with foil.

Bake 45-50 minutes; uncover carefully, removing foil from back to front to allow hot steam to escape; bake 15-20 minutes longer until fruit is bubbly and crumbs are golden brown. Serve warm with cinnamon or other ice cream.

NOTE: Cinnamon ice cream can be found in shops or, to make your own version, blend 1 teaspoon ground cinnamon into a pint of softened, good-quality vanilla ice cream.

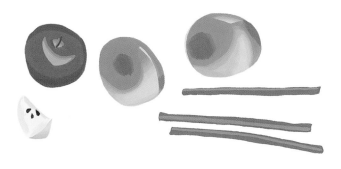

LOEWS LE CONCORDE HOTEL

Québec City, Canada

EXECUTIVE CHEF MARIO MARTEL

Until his appointment as Executive Chef for **Loews Le Concorde,** Mario Martel always owned the restaurants where he cooked. During twenty years in the restaurant business, Chef Martel has won awards and accolades for his pioneer work in creating a cuisine that blends classical French and regional Québeçoise elements with contemporary style.

Committed to using the best regional products— from dairy to seafood— Chef Martel is known for his varied use of salmon…more than 20 different dishes!

With a spectacular 360-degree panoramic view of Québec Ciy, Loews Le Concorde's rooftop restaurant, L'Astral offers an eclectic menu that reflects the region's international influences.

Overlooking the Saint Lawrence River and just steps from the old walled city, the hotel features 422 rooms, 2 suites, and two duplex penthouse suites. A health club and heated outdoor pool for seasonal use are available for recreation, while a business center and 18 meeting and banquet rooms can accommodate meetings and social functions for groups up to 1,000.

Salmon has always been a regal dish.
—James Beard

QUEBEC CHANTERELLE TART
WITH TOMATOES AND
AGED CHEDDAR

Serves 4

1 frozen puff pastry sheet (from 17¼-ounce package), thawed according to package directions

3 medium, vine-ripened tomatoes (about 6 ounces each)

1 tablespoon olive oil, plus 1 teaspoon

    Salt and freshly ground black pepper

    Pinch of sugar

3 tablespoons unsalted butter

¾ cup finely chopped shallots

8 ounces Chanterelle or Shiitaki mushrooms, wiped clean (stems of Shiitake removed and discarded if using) and coarsely chopped

    Aged Cheddar cheese for topping

½ cup dry white wine

1 cup heavy cream

    Snipped chives for garnish

Unfold thawed pastry onto a lightly floured surface. Roll out to a 10½-inch square. Cut out four 5-inch rounds. Place on a large baking sheet lined with parchment paper. Return to freezer.

Preheat oven to 400°F.

Score an "X" in stem end of each tomato. Plunge into a saucepan of boiling water for 1 minute, then place in a bowl of ice water to stop cooking. Peel, core and quarter tomatoes; remove pulpy center and seeds with a small knife. Place tomato quarters in a shallow baking dish large enough to hold them in a single layer with one teaspoon olive oil, salt, pepper and pinch of sugar; toss to combine. Arrange in single layer and bake 10-15 minutes until softened but not mushy. Cool on wire rack.*

Remove pastry from freezer and bake at 400° F. until puffed and golden brown, about 15 minutes. Cool on a wire rack.

In a large skillet over medium-high heat, melt 2 tablespoons butter with remaining 1 tablespoon oil. Add ½ cup of the shallots and the chopped mushrooms; sauté until mushrooms are soft and just beginning to stick to skillet, about 5-7 minutes. Turn into a bowl; cool. Set skillet aside but do not wipe out.

To assemble tarts, divide mushrooms and place in a mound in center of each cooled, baked pastry round. Arrange 3 tomato quarters around mushrooms. Return to 400° F. oven and bake 5 minutes until hot. Remove from oven and, using a vegetable peeler, shave several shards of Cheddar over each tart. Return to oven and bake additional 3 minutes or until cheese has melted.

While tarts are baking, melt remaining 1 tablespoon butter in skillet. Add remaining ¼ cup shallots; sauté over medium-high heat until tender, about 3 minutes.

Add wine and reduce to half, about 2-3 minutes. Stir in heavy cream; cook and stir until thickened, about 5-7 minutes; keep warm.

Place tarts on individual serving dishes; spoon sauce around and top with snipped chives.

* Recipe can be prepared in advance up to this point.

ATLANTIC SALMON
WITH CREAMY POLENTA AND
SHIITAKE MUSHROOMS

In a large skillet over medium heat, sauté shallots in 1 tablespoon oil until translucent, about 1 minute. Add mushrooms, sauté until mushrooms are soft and just beginning to brown, about 4 minutes. Add chicken stock or broth and bring to a boil over high heat. Gradually add polenta, whisking constantly, until combined and mixture begins to "plop."

Remove from heat; cover and let stand, off heat, 3 minutes. Stir in herbs. Season with salt and pepper to taste.

Preheat oven to 200°F.

Heat a 12-inch nonstick skillet over medium-high heat until it is quite hot, about 5 minutes. Add 1 tablespoon oil to skillet and cook the salmon fillets, in batches, 3-4 minutes per side, depending upon their thickness, season with salt and pepper as they cook. They should be nicely browned, but not cooked through. Remove the cooked fillets to a heat-proof platter and place in oven to keep warm.

While salmon is cooking, drop snow peas into small saucepan of boiling water. When water comes back to a boil, drain snow peas and keep warm.

In a small bowl, whisk together the remaining 4 tablespoons oil with the lemon juice.

To serve, place a generous amount of the polenta in the center of serving plate. Top with a salmon fillet, sprinkle with snow peas and drizzle on some of the lemon-oil emulsion.

Serves 6

2	tablespoons finely chopped shallots
6	tablespoons olive oil
3	ounces Shiitake mushrooms, washed, trimmed and coarsely chopped (1 cup), stems removed and discarded
4	cups chicken stock or canned low-sodium chicken broth
1	cup instant polenta
1	tablespoon snipped fresh chives
1	teaspoon chopped fresh thyme leaves
	Salt and freshly ground black pepper
6	fresh Atlantic salmon fillets (about 6 ounces each), skin removed
2	ounces fresh snow peas, julienned
1½	tablespoons fresh lemon juice

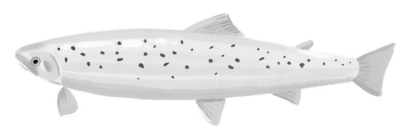

MAPLE BUTTER CREPES

Serves 6

- ¾ cup all-purpose flour
- 2 tablespoons granulated sugar
- 3 tablespoons unsalted butter, melted
- 3 large eggs, at room temperature
- ½ teaspoon vanilla
- 1 cup milk
- ½ cup (1 stick) unsalted butter
- ½ cup maple sugar
- ½ cup maple syrup
- Confectioners sugar

In a medium bowl, combine flour, sugar, 2 tablespoons melted butter, eggs, vanilla and ½ cup milk; beat with a wire whisk or rotary beater until smooth. Beat in the remaining milk until mixture is well blended. Cover and refrigerate at least 1 hour.

Slowly heat a 7-inch crepe pan until a drop of water sizzles and rolls off. For each crepe, brush pan lightly with remaining melted butter. Pour in 3 tablespoons batter, rotating pan quickly to spread batter completely over bottom of pan. Cook until top is set and underside is golden; turn, brown other side. Stack crepes between waxed paper. Makes 12 crepes.

In a large skillet or chafing dish, melt the ½ cup butter. Add maple sugar and syrup. Cook and stir until bubbly and well blended. Add crepes, one at a time; turn and fold each crepe in half, then in half again and push to the edge of the pan. Cook over low heat a few minutes until heated through.

Serve 2 crepes per person with some of the maple butter sauce. Dust with confectioners sugar.

LOEWS MIAMI BEACH HOTEL
South Beach, Florida

The first all-new hotel to open in Miami Beach in 30 years, LOEWS MIAMI BEACH HOTEL features 800 rooms, 85,000 square feet of flexible meeting space, and a

host of recreational amenities and retail opportunities. A diverse and tempting roster of food and beverage choices will be found in its restaurants and lounges. These include the chic and sophisticated GAUCHO ROOM, an Argentinean steakhouse with *al fresco* dining; PRESTON's, a hip dining spot for American cuisine flavored with a South Florida flair; the NAUTILUS, a fun and casual poolside grill; the cozy GAUCHO BAR, with wraparound piano bar; HEMISPHERE LOUNGE for cocktails and conversation, and the SoBe COFFEE BAR for fresh roasts and exotic blends.

FLORIDA ROCK SHRIMP
AND GRILLED SCALLION EMPANADITAS WITH
MANGO JICAMA SLAW

Serves 6

Mango Jicama Slaw (recipe follows)

1   cup all-purpose flour

1   cup yellow cornmeal

1   teaspoon salt

½   cup vegetable shortening

6   tablespoons ice water

3   large scallions

1   tablespoon olive oil, plus some to brush over scallions

1   tablespoon unseeded minced jalapeño pepper

1½   teaspoons minced fresh garlic

7   ounces rock shrimp, drained, patted dry with paper towels and coarsely chopped

2   tablespoons minced fresh cilantro

Make Mango Jicama Slaw and refrigerate.

In a large bowl, combine flour, cornmeal and salt. Cut in shortening with a pastry blender until mixture resembles coarse crumbs. Add water and stir with a fork until the mixture is moistened. Gather dough together and shape into a ball. Cut in half, shape each half into a ball and flatten slightly into a disk. Wrap in plastic wrap and refrigerate at least 2 hours until firm enough to roll out.

Meanwhile, heat a top-of-the-stove grill over high heat. Brush scallions with oil and grill 5 minutes, turning frequently, until slightly charred; cool and chop.

In a medium skillet over high heat, heat 1 tablespoon oil; add jalapeño and garlic and sauté 30 seconds. Add chopped shrimp; cook and toss 1 minute just until shrimp turn slightly pink and begin to release their juices. Add chopped scallions and cilantro; mix to combine. Turn into a small bowl and cool. Cover and refrigerate until cold.

Working with one half of the dough at a time, roll out to a ⅛-inch thickness between sheets of waxed paper. Flip dough over with waxed paper for even rolling and if paper is wrinkling, lift off to loosen. Cut the dough into rounds with a 3-inch cutter.

Remove excess dough from rounds and save trimmings. Using waxed paper to aid, remove rounds to two large baking sheets. Repeat with remaining dough. Reroll trimmings until you have 24 rounds.

Drain off any liquid from shrimp. Place about 1 teaspoon of the shrimp filling onto rounds. Bring edges together to form a semi-circle and seal tightly with thumb and forefinger. Place back onto baking sheets and press edges of each empanadita with tines of a fork. Chill in refrigerator for 15 minutes.

Meanwhile, preheat oven to 400°F.

Bake empanaditas 12-15 minutes or until firm and slightly golden. To serve, mound about ⅓ cup of the Mango Jicama Slaw in center of each serving plate. Place 4 hot empanaditas around the slaw. Serve at once.

MANGO JICAMA
SLAW

Peel mango. Using a mandoline or vegetable slicer with a julienne blade, julienne mango flesh, or remove mango flesh in one piece from either side of pit and cut into thin strips. Combine in a medium bowl with jicama, red pepper, oil, lime juice and cilantro. Add salt and pepper to taste. Cover and refrigerate until ready to use.

Serves 6

1 medium-size ripe mango (about 1 pound)

½ cup peeled and julienned jicama

¼ cup julienned red bell pepper

2 tablespoons extra-virgin olive oil

1 tablespoon fresh lime juice

1 tablespoon minced fresh cilantro

Salt and freshly ground black pepper

BEEF IN
CHIMICHURRI SAUCE

Serves 6

1   cup olive oil

¼   cup champagne vinegar

¼   cup fresh lime juice

¼   cup chopped fresh oregano

¼   cup chopped fresh parsley

3   garlic cloves, chopped

1   teaspoon red pepper flakes

½   teaspoon cayenne

     Salt and freshly ground black pepper

1   2¼-pound beef filet (tender-loin) or loin strip roast, trimmed and tied [see NOTE]

     Apple or pecan wood chips

In a small bowl, make Chimichurri Sauce by combining olive oil, champagne vinegar, lime juice, oregano, parsley, garlic, red pepper flakes, cayenne and salt and pepper to taste. You will have 1½ cups.

Place meat in a large, heavy, zip-top plastic bag. Pour over ¾ cup of Chimichurri Sauce. Remove air from the bag and close. Squeeze bag to coat meat with the sauce and refrigerate 2 hours. Cover and refrigerate remaining Chimichurri Sauce in a bowl.

Remove meat and the reserved sauce from refrigerator at least 30 minutes before grilling.

Prepare a medium-hot fire in a covered charcoal or gas grill. Soak the wood chips in cold water for at least 30 minutes. Just before cooking, toss the wet chips onto the hot coals or add to a gas grill according to the manufacturer's directions.

Remove meat from the bag and place on grill; reserve marinade. Grill the meat, turning occasionally, basting with the marinade from the bag, until the outside of the meat is well browned and the inside is cooked to the desired degree of doneness, allowing 10-12 minutes per pound. The internal temperature of the meat should register 125°F. for medium-rare or 135°F. for medium on an instant-read thermometer. Let rest 10 minutes before slicing. Spoon Chimichurri Sauce from bowl over the meat. Serve with garlic and oregano-roasted potatoes and a tossed green salad.

NOTE: If using a loin strip roast, leave a ½-inch layer of fat around the roast. For individual steaks, have butcher cut the meat into 6-ounce portions, about 1½ inches thick and tied with butchers' twine. Sear 2 minutes on each side and continue grilling 4-5 minutes on each side to desired doneness.

MANGO AND
WHITE RUM SORBET

In a medium saucepan, combine water, sugar and corn syrup. Cook and stir over medium-low heat until sugar dissolves. Remove from heat and cool to room temperature.

Peel and seed mangoes; cut into large chunks directly into food processor bowl.

Add lime juice; puree until smooth. Pour into large bowl. Stir in cooled sugar syrup and rum; cover and refrigerate until very cold, about 3 hours.

Pour mixture into canister of an ice cream maker and freeze according to manufacturer's directions. Or pour mixture into a 9-inch square metal pan. Freeze until solid, about 6 hours, stirring occasionally to bring firm edges of the mango sorbet into the soft center. Break into chunks and process until smooth in a food processor. Spoon into plastic container and refreeze until firm.

Makes 3 cups

2 cups water

2/3 cup sugar

2/3 cup light corn syrup

2 large, very ripe, soft mangos (1 pound each)

2 tablespoons fresh lime juice

1/4 cup white rum

DIRECTORY OF LOEWS HOTELS

Loews Annapolis Hotel
126 West Street
Annapolis, MD 21401
410-263-7777
410-263-0084 (fax)
e-mail loewsannapolis@loewshotels.com

Loews Coronado Bay Resort
4000 Coronado Bay Road
Coronado, CA 92118
619-424-4000
619-424-4400 (fax)
e-mail loewscoronadobay@loewshotels.com

Loews Giorgio Hotel
4150 East Mississippi Avenue
Denver, CO 80222
303-782-9300
303-782-6542 (fax)
e-mail loewsgiorgio@loewshotels.com

Loews L'Enfant Plaza Hotel
480 L'Enfant Plaza SW
Washington D.C. 20024
202-484-1000
202-646-4456 (fax)
e-mail loewslenfantplaza@loewshotels.com

Loews New York Hotel
569 Lexington Avenue
New York, NY 10022
212-752-7000
212-758-6930 (fax)
e-mail loewsnewyork@loewshotels.com

The Regency Hotel
540 Park Avenue
New York, NY 10021
212-759-4100
212-826-5674 (fax)
e-mail regency@loewshotels.com

Loews Santa Monica Beach Hotel
1700 Ocean Avenue
Santa Monica, CA 90401
310-458-6700
310-458-6761 (fax)
e-mail loewssantamonicabeach@loewshotels.com

Loews Vanderbilt Plaza Hotel
2100 West End Avenue
Nashville, TN 37203
615-320-1700
615-320-5019 (fax)
e-mail loewsvanderbilt@loewshotels.com

Loews Ventana Canyon Resort
7000 North Resort Drive
Tucson, AZ 85715
520-299-2020
520-299-6832 (fax)
e-mail loewsventanacanyon@loewshotels.com

Loews Le Concorde Hotel
1225 Place Montcalm
Québec City, Canada G1R 4W6
418-647-2222
418- 647-4710 (fax)
e-mail loewsleconcorde@loewshotels.com

Loews Hotel Vogue
1425 Rue de la Montagne
Montréal, Canada H3G 1Z3
514-285-5555
514-849-8903 (fax)
e-mail loewsvogue@loewshotels.com

Loews Monte Carlo Hotel
12 Avenue des Spelugues
Monte Carlo, B.P. 179
98007 Monaco
011-377-93-5065-00
011-377-93-3001-57 (fax)
e-mail loewsmontecarlo@loewshotels.com

Loews Miami Beach Hotel (opening October 1998)
1601 Collins Avenue (at 16th Street)
Miami Beach, FL 33139
305-604-1601
305-531-8677 (fax)
e-mail loewsmiamibeach@loewshotels.com

Loews Portofino Bay Resort (opening in 1999)
A Loews Hotel
Universal Florida
1000 Universal Studio Plaza
Orlando, FL 32819
407-248-2920
407-248-2960 (fax)

Loews Philadelphia Hotel (opening in mid-1999)
(PSFS Building)
12 South 12th Street
Philadelphia, PA 19107
215-351-0700
215-351-0702 (fax)

Loews Hotels
667 Madison Avenue
New York, NY 10021
212-521-2000
212-935-6796 (fax)
www.loewshotels.com

INDEX